Greater London History Sources

Volume 2

Middlesex - part 1

Series editors
Richard Knight
Kathleen Shawcross

Guildhall Library Publications
in association with the
Greater London Archives Network

British Library Cataloguing in Publication Data.
A catalogue record for this book is available from
the British Library

Published by the Corporation of London
Guildhall Library Publications
in association with the Greater London Archives Network

Corporation of London
Guildhall Library Publications
Guildhall Library
Aldermanbury
LONDON
EC2V 7HH

ISBN 0 900422 51 3 Hardback
ISBN 0 900422 52 1 Paperback

Printed by Hobbs the Printers, Totton, Hampshire

Contents

Acknowledgements

This guide has been many years in gestation. The project was originally conceived by the Association of London Chief Librarians. Further work was done by the Local Studies Group of the Library Association, and latterly the project has been co-ordinated by the Greater London Archives Network (G.L.A.N.). The detailed editing and preparation of this volume have been undertaken under the auspices of G.L.A.N., using information supplied by individual contributors.

The editors are grateful to the many people who have helped in the production of this second volume. There are too many to mention everyone by name but we are especially grateful to our colleagues in G.L.A.N. particularly Chris Bennett, Archivist for the London Borough of Croydon, and to the archives and local studies staff of the London boroughs of Barnet, Camden, Ealing, Hackney, Hammersmith and Fulham, Hillingdon and Hounslow. Without their support and assistance this volume could not have been brought to completion.

The illustrations in this volume are reproduced with the permission of the contributing boroughs and the Corporation of London. The financial support of the Corporation of London is also gratefully acknowledged.

Cover image shows 'Collins Cottage (later called Wyldes Farm) at North End, Hampstead, looking north towards Barnet' , 1830 by C. Barnard. Reproduced by permission of the Camden Local Studies and Archives Centre.

Greater London Archives Network

Founded in 1982, G.L.A.N. provides a forum for professional activities, discussion and mutual support for members working in a wide range of record offices and libraries - ranging from large local authority repositories to smaller offices and specialist services. It offers a programme of training events and meetings for members, encourages high standards of record keeping and promotes public access through the publication of directories, guides and surveys.

The series editors are Richard Knight, Principal Offcer: Local Studies and Archives for the London Borough of Camden, and Kathleen Shawcross, Borough Archivist and Local Studies Manager for the London Borough of Sutton.

Introduction to the series

Greater London History Sources is a guide to printed and visual materials, archives and manuscripts held in publicly-funded local record offices and local studies collections in and around London. In a series of volumes, it will cover the City of London and the 32 London Boroughs which together make up the area known as Greater London. The extent of this area, and the boundaries of the London Boroughs, are shown on the map on p. 11.

The multiplicity of record offices and libraries in London means that archive materials in particular are not always held in the location where they might be expected. It is hoped that this guide will help researchers in locating source material which they know to exist, and will also alert them to the existence of materials of which they might otherwise have been unaware.

Besides London Borough local studies libraries and record offices, the City of London and London Metropolitan Archives were invited to make contributions to the guide, as were record offices in adjoining counties and some other repositories holding relevant materials such as hospital archives. While it is known that national bodies such as the British Library and the National Archives (formerly the Public Record Office) hold much material relating to London history, the scale of the project made it impossible to attempt to include full details of their holdings.

Each contributing record office or library was asked to submit a return based on a standard questionnaire. The information in the guide has therefore been provided by the individual contributors, and the degree of detail supplied has been largely left to their discretion. Some inconsistencies in depth of description between one contributor and another are therefore inevitable. However the returns have been edited into a common style, and for this the series editors are responsible.

Arrangement of the guide

Within each volume of *Greater London History Sources*, the contributing libraries and record offices are listed in alphabetical order. A standard arrangement is used to describe the holdings of each contributor, and an outline of this is given below.

Brief details of each library or record office are provided at the head of its entry in the guide: the address, telephone and fax numbers; e-mail address and website; and access arrangements. The guide gives days of opening at the time of going to press and states whether a prior appointment is required or recommended. (For more detailed information about opening hours and access arrangements users are referred to Archon, the on-line directory of archives services in the U.K. on the National Archives website at www.nationalarchives.gov.uk/archon).

Information is also given at the head of each entry about catalogues and indexes, published research guides and services that are available to users of the library or record office.

This is followed by a description of its holdings: printed materials are described first, followed by visual and audio-visual materials and collections of museum objects; the final sections describe holdings of archives and manuscripts. Where non-London archives are held, these too are described.

Users of the guide may find it helpful to note the following points:

- Only a brief description is given of printed materials, whether local or national, which are widely available. Details of standard printed sources on the history of London are available on the London's Past On-line website produced by the Centre for Metropolitan History at www.history.ac.uk/cmh/lpol. In Greater London History Sources, rarer printed items such as local newspapers and directories, which may not be readily available elsewhere, are described in more detail than books and pamphlets.

- In describing archival holdings the guide provides a summary of each significant group of archives. In most cases, though not all, a more detailed list should be available in the library or record office concerned. Published guides or lists have been mentioned where details are available.

- For reasons of space it has been necessary to exclude many smaller or less significant deposits of personal, family and estate papers; users can assume that many contributors will hold substantial numbers of title deeds and similar documents relating to their locality. Business archives which comprise only title deeds, and/or partnership deeds dated after 1800 have also not been included. Details of these records should be available from the library or record office concerned.

- Many libraries and borough record offices hold microform or photographic copies of original records, such as parish registers deposited in London Metropolitan Archives, public records held in the National Archives, or archives held elsewhere. Such copies are only listed in the guide where the original records are held in a location which may not permit easy access.

- Virtually all record offices and local studies collections can be assumed to hold microfilm copies of census returns for their locality from 1841 to 1901. Many local archives will also hold transcripts of records, such as parish registers, and of monumental inscriptions.

Many archives and libraries will also provide access to the Internet either free or for a small charge.

The description of the holdings of each library or record office is arranged in sections as follows:
1. Books, pamphlets and periodicals
2. Special collections of printed material
3. Newspapers
4. Cuttings collections
5. Directories
6. Electoral registers and poll books
7. Illustrations
8. Maps
9. Audio-visual items
10. Collections of museum objects
11. Local authority records and records of predecessor authorities
12. Local records of central government
13. Records of other public authorities
14. Records of courts of law

15. Records of dioceses, archdeaconries and rural deaneries, cathedrals and other ecclesiastical jurisdictions
16. Records of parishes
17. Records of non-Anglican places of worship
18. Records of religious organisations
19. Records of livery companies and related organisations
20. Records of almshouses
21. Records of hospitals, asylums and dispensaries
22. Records of orphanages, refuges and penitentiaries
23. Records of schools and colleges
24. Records of prisons
25. Records of other institutions
26. Records of cemeteries and crematoria
27. Records of fire and salvage brigades
28. Records of military and armed bodies
29. Records of associations, clubs and societies
30. Records of theatres and cinemas
31. Records of business associations and market exchanges
32. Records of fairs and markets
33. Records of businesses
34. Family and personal papers and records of private estates
35. Manorial records
36. Manuscripts and manuscript collections
37. Antiquarians' collections
38. Copies of source material held elsewhere

Where no material of a particular type is held, the relevant section is omitted from the guide.

Access to sources

Access by means of a personal visit to the record offices and libraries covered in this guide is generally free of charge. Most record offices and libraries will answer simple enquiries by post, e-mail, telephone or fax, and this service is usually also free of charge; however more complex postal and telephone enquiries may be charged for, or may be referred to a professional record agent. No library or record office is able to undertake unlimited research on behalf of enquirers.

Most of the source materials listed in this guide are available to researchers without special permission or other formality. In some cases, however, timed appointments, advance notice of visits and/or proof of identity may be required, or there may be restrictions imposed for reasons of confidentiality. Where any such restrictions are known to apply, they are indicated in the guide. The Freedom of Information Act (2000) provides general access to all types of recorded information. From January 2005 some restrictions noted in this guide may cease to exist. Researchers should contact individual record offices to verify access.

Virtually all record offices and libraries reserve the right to produce materials in microform copy, and to restrict or prohibit access to the originals, particularly in the case of heavily used or fragile items.

Most record offices and libraries offer photocopying and other reprographic services, but copyright law means that some parts of their holdings may not be available for copying. Other restrictions may also be applied, particularly where fragile materials are concerned. Fees are always charged for copying.

The growth of London

The City of London [1] was probably established as an urban settlement by the Romans in the first century A.D.; it has been a distinct local government entity since before the Norman conquest.

The London Boroughs, however, are of much more recent origin. The areas which they cover were formerly in the counties of Middlesex, Essex, Hertfordshire, Kent and Surrey. In the middle ages, apart from a few suburban streets outside the City gates, these areas were almost entirely rural. By the seventeenth century, however, urbanisation had spread to Westminster, Holborn, Southwark and the areas adjoining the City in what became the East End. In the eighteenth century the built-up area expanded to include such places as Marylebone, Lambeth and Shoreditch, and by the end of the nineteenth century it had reached as far as the former villages of Hornsey, Tottenham and Walthamstow in the north, Chiswick in the west and Streatham and Sydenham in the south.

Continued expansion in the years between the first and second world wars engulfed the small towns of outer Middlesex such as Enfield and Hounslow; south of the River Thames, Kingston, Croydon and Bromley were also caught up in the spread of London. When suburban growth was halted by the 'Green Belt' legislation of 1938 and 1947, the metropolitan area reached from Barnet to Banstead and from Uxbridge to Upminster, an area of some 600 square miles.

Administrative history of Greater London

Until the nineteenth century local government in the London area, outside the City, followed broadly the pattern of the rest of England. Responsibility at local level rested with the vestry of each parish, subject to the general supervision of the county Justices of the Peace. Originally purely ecclesiastical bodies, the vestries accumulated a variety of civil duties between the sixteenth and nineteenth centuries. Within the City, parish vestries followed the normal pattern in having oversight of poor relief, but had fewer other powers than their counterparts elsewhere. After the Poor Law Amendment Act (1834), parishes both in the City and elsewhere were grouped into Unions for purposes of poor relief; for other purposes, however, the traditional methods of parish administration remained unaffected by this act.

In the course of the nineteenth century it was recognised that the growth of metropolitan London had brought with it a need for local government reform. Local boards and trusts had already been established for various purposes, including about 300 for paving. By the middle of the century there were a number of other administrative bodies in the parts of London outside the City, including a Metropolitan Commission of Sewers (created in 1848 by the amalgamation of seven previous sewer commissions). The Metropolitan Commission of Sewers and various other bodies were superseded by a Metropolitan Board of Works established in 1856 under the Metropolis Local Management Act (1855). In the more central parts of London fifteen district boards were also created, while elsewhere additional powers were given to the vestries.

1. An account of the administrative history of the City of London is given in volume 1.

Under the Local Government Act (1888) the urbanised parts of Middlesex, Kent and Surrey were detached from those counties to form a new County of London. The Metropolitan Board of Works was abolished in 1889, its powers being transferred to the new London County Council. District boards within the London County Council area were abolished under the London Government Act (1899), and parish vestries within that area were also disbanded except where they survived with ecclesiastical functions. In their place, 28 Metropolitan Boroughs were created in 1900.

Various other bodies were established in the late nineteenth century to administer particular local services, such as Local Commissioners for Libraries. Most of these were subsequently taken over by the Metropolitan Borough Councils or the London County Council. The London School Board, founded in 1870, was subsumed into the London County Council in 1903.

In the remaining parts of the counties surrounding London new county councils were also established in 1889, largely replacing the role of the Justices of the Peace in local administration. Three towns near the metropolis (Croydon and West and East Ham) became county boroughs, with county powers of their own which placed them outside the jurisdiction of the county councils. Local boards or sanitary authorities which had been set up in some places under the Local Government Board Act (1871) and Public Health Act (1872) were superseded by the Urban and Rural District Councils established by the Local Government Act (1894) in areas outside the County of London and the county boroughs. Civil parishes were also created in 1894, with parish councils taking over the civil powers of the vestries in rural districts. The powers of school boards, set up in 1870, were transferred to the county councils under the Education Act (1902).

In the twentieth century the continued growth of London led to further administrative changes. During the first half of the century many of the urban districts in Middlesex, Essex, Kent and Surrey became municipal, i.e. non-county, boroughs (joining Kingston-upon-Thames which had enjoyed borough status since c.1200). [2]

Following the London Government Act (1963) a new County of Greater London was formed, comprising the City, the whole of the former County of London, almost all of Middlesex and parts of Essex, Surrey, Kent and Hertfordshire. The London and Middlesex County Councils were abolished, the few parts of Middlesex excluded from Greater London being transferred to Hertfordshire or Surrey. A Greater London Council was established in 1965, with its headquarters in the County Hall of the former London County Council on the south bank of the Thames. At the same time the 32 London Boroughs were created by amalgamating the previously existing borough and district councils. An Inner London Education Authority was formed to manage schools and other educational services in the area of the former County of London, while in the outer parts of Greater London educational powers were assigned to the London Borough Councils.

In 1986 the Greater London Council was abolished. Many of its powers were transferred to the London Boroughs, while others went to central government or to other bodies. The Inner London Education Authority was abolished in 1990, its powers being transferred to the Borough Councils of inner London. In 2000 a new Greater London Authority was created run by a directly elected mayor and an assembly.

2. Apart from the City, Kingston-upon-Thames was the only ancient incorporated borough in what is now Greater London. An account of its administrative history, which does not wholly conform to the pattern described here, will be given in a later volume.

Editorial conventions

It is difficult to devise a consistent system for recording place names in Greater London in a guide to sources covering nine centuries. The London postal districts are of relatively recent origin and are not appropriate when describing sources from earlier periods. Streets and localities in the City of London, Westminster, Holborn, Finsbury and Southwark are indicated as such; except in volume 1, where only addresses in Westminster, Holborn, Finsbury and Southwark are noted in this way and place names in the City of London are not further defined. Addresses in Stepney are identified by the names of the former hamlets (Mile End, Shadwell, Wapping, etc.). References to other localities are assigned to the appropriate ancient parish, village or town (and, if they are outside the former L.C.C. area, to their historic county).

Where the guide gives the covering dates of a series, significant gaps in coverage are either specified in detail or indicated by use of the word 'gaps'. Smaller gaps, however, may not be noted. Where no gaps are indicated, it should not be inferred that a series is necessarily wholly complete.

Dates before 1752 (when the calendar was changed to establish the beginning of the year as 1 January rather than 25 March) are shown in the guide as 'new style' dates. For example, 24 March 1700/1 is noted as 1701.

Volume 2: Middlesex – part 1

Volume 2 describes the holdings of 7 of the 15 London boroughs which lay wholly or partly in the former County of Middlesex. Parts of the London Borough of Barnet lay within the County of Hertfordshire.

Many other records relating to Middlesex are held in London Metropolitan Archives and to Hertfordshire in Hertfordshire Archives and Local Studies. These are not described in this volume. Details of the record offices are given below:

London Metropolitan Archives
40 Northampton Road
London
EC1R 0HB
Tel: 020 7332 3820
Website: www.cityoflondon.gov.uk/lma

Hertfordshire Archives and Local Studies
County Hall
Hertford
SG13 8DE
Tel: 01438 737333
Website: www.hertsdirect.org

Volume 1 described archives and other sources relating to the City of London. The holdings of the other London boroughs in the former County of Middlesex will be described in later volumes.

Map of Greater London

Part of John Warburton's map of Middlesex, published 1749

London Borough of Barnet

Barnet Local Studies and Archives
80 Daws Lane
Mill Hill
London
NW7 4SL

Tel:
020-8959 6657

E-mail:
library.archives@barnet.gov.uk

Website:
www.barnet.gov.uk/localstudies

Location:
Disabled Access
Toilets.

Nearest station:
Mill Hill (Thameslink) 1,000 metres
Mill Hill East (Northern Line) and Edgware (Northern Line). Catch 240 bus from either station.

Parking:
Adjacent free car park.

Days of opening:
Tuesday, Wednesday, Thursday, Friday and two Saturdays a month by appointment.

Administrative history:
The London Borough of Barnet comprises the former boroughs of Finchley and Hendon and the urban districts of Barnet, East Barnet and Friern Barnet. Before 1965 the urban districts of Barnet and East Barnet were in Hertfordshire; the rest of the borough was in Middlesex.

The ancient parishes within the London Borough of Barnet were: Edgware, Finchley, Friern Barnet, Hendon and Monken Hadley (Middlesex); and Chipping Barnet, East Barnet and Totteridge (Hertfordshire). The parishes of Hendon and Edgware were covered by the Hendon Poor Law Union; the remaining parishes were covered by the Barnet Union.

Holdings:

The Archives and Local Studies Centre holdings are based upon the records of current and previous administrations, the Hendon Libraries local collection, begun in 1932, and the Finchley Libraries local collection, begun in 1944.

Catalogues and indexes:

Integrated card index for the archives and local studies collections, divided into subject, place and personal name sections covering the whole borough. Separate indexes for maps, local artists and slides. Computerised finding aids in progress.

Services:

Photocopying facilities.
Microfilm reader/printer.
PC/Internet access.

Related collections held elsewhere:

BARNET AND DISTRICT LOCAL HISTORY SOCIETY
Barnet Museum
31 Wood Street
Barnet
Herts
(tel: 020-8440 8066)
Website: www.barnetmuseum.co.uk
Printed works, maps, directories, photographs and postcards relating to Chipping Barnet and East Barnet.

FINCHLEY SOCIETY
Website: www.finchleysociety.org.uk
Postcards and photographs and other printed material relating to Finchley.

1. BOOKS, PAMPHLETS AND PERIODICALS

Histories of all areas of the present borough. Biographies of people connected with the area.

Parish magazines, school journals, publications from local residents and amenity groups and periodicals concerned with archaeology and local history.

Victoria County History:
Middlesex vol. 4 - Edgware
Middlesex vol. 5 - Hendon and Monken Hadley
Middlesex vol. 6 - Finchley and Friern Barnet
Middlesex vol. 9 - Childs Hill

2. SPECIAL COLLECTIONS OF PRINTED MATERIAL

HENDON AERODROME
Collection of books, programmes of air shows and pageants and material on the aerodrome and people connected with it from 1911.

3. NEWSPAPERS

BARNET PRESS 1861-1914 (gaps).
Later editions in Hendon Library.

HENDON AND FINCHLEY TIMES 1876-1914.
Later editions in Hendon Library.

FINCHLEY PRESS 1895-1960; continued as FINCHLEY TIMES AND GUARDIAN 1961-1964.

4. CUTTINGS COLLECTIONS

A collection of loose cuttings and 23 volumes taken mainly from the local press relating to Chipping Barnet, Hendon and Finchley areas in the early 20th century; very narrow in scope, covering local government, elections and education.

5. DIRECTORIES

5.1 Court guides

BOYLE'S FASHIONABLE COURT AND COUNTRY GUIDE
1844, 1847.

CLAYTON'S COURT GUIDE TO THE ENVIRONS OF LONDON
1830.

5.2 London, county and general directories

LONDON
Post Office (Various publishers until 1836; from 1837 published by Kelly's).
1843, 1851, 1866.

MIDDLESEX AND HERTS
Provincial business directories.
1949/50.

MIDDLESEX AND HERTS
Town and Country (trade directory).
1954/55.

5.3 Local directories

BARNET, FINCHLEY, HENDON ETC.
1st edition Hutchings and Crowsley; later editions by Kelly's.
1886/87, 1911/12, 1922-1923, 1926-1939.

BARNET AND NEW BARNET
Kelly's.
1890, 1923, 1926, 1931, 1937.

BARNET AND EAST BARNET
Borough Directories Ltd (From 1964 published as London Borough of Barnet Directory vol. 3).
1961-1969.

EDGWARE
Kelly's.
1930-1939.

EDGWARE, MILL HILL AND BURNT OAK
Kemps.
1959-1961.

ENFIELD
London and Provincial Publications.
1953/54.

FINCHLEY
Kelly's.
1926, 1930-1939.

FINCHLEY
London and Provincial Publications.
1949-1954.

FINCHLEY BOROUGH
Borough Directories Ltd (From 1964 published as London Borough of Barnet Directory vol. 2).
1961-1970.

HAMPSTEAD AND HIGHGATE
Kelly's.
1938-1940.

HAMPSTEAD
Borough Directories Ltd (From 1964 published as London Borough of Camden Directory vol. 1).
1959/60, 1961, 1965/66, 1970.

HAMPSTEAD GARDEN SUBURB
Co-Partnership.
1915.

HENDON BOROUGH
C. Odell Ltd.
1904, 1905, 1908.

HENDON
Kelly's.
1926-1939.

HENDON INCLUDING CRICKLEWOOD, EDGWARE AND GOLDER'S GREEN
London and Provincial Directories.
1950/51, 1952/53.

HENDON
Borough Directories Ltd (From 1964 published as London Borough of Barnet Directory Vol. 1).
1959/60, 1964-1970.

HORNSEY
Kelly's.
1928, 1939.

KILBURN INCLUDING WILLESDEN, CRICKLEWOOD AND WEST HAMPSTEAD
Kelly's.
1939.

MIDDLESEX
Kelly's.
Barnet, Finchley and Southgate sections.
1917, 1920, 1922.

SOUTHGATE
Kent Service Ltd.
1958.

TOTTERIDGE
Kelly's.
1937.

WEMBLEY
Curleys.
1968.

WOOD GREEN
Kelly's.
1938.

5.4 Telephone directories

5.4.2 Local areas

BARNET
1952, 1953, 1973/74, 1977, 1980-1983, 1985/86, 1988 to date.

FINCHLEY, BARNET AND DISTRICT
1928.

EDGWARE AND DISTRICT
1972.

6. ELECTORAL REGISTERS

BARNET
1930, 1936, 1957-1958, 1960-1965.

EAST BARNET
1939, 1948-1962.

FINCHLEY
1908, 1921, 1924, 1936-1939, 1945-1965.

HENDON
1901, 1903, 1905, 1906, 1908-1910, 1912-1928, 1930-1939, 1945-1965.

LONDON BOROUGH OF BARNET
1966 to date.

7. ILLUSTRATIONS

About 2,000 drawings, paintings and prints covering all parts of the present borough with the emphasis on Finchley and Hendon in the nineteenth century.

About 5,000 photographs and postcards from the later nineteenth century onwards covering all parts of the present borough. A photographic survey was undertaken between 1982 and 1986 covering most parts of the borough except Finchley and Hampstead Garden Suburb.

Small but growing collection of 35mm slides which is used for lectures.

8. MAPS

8.1 General maps

The earliest detailed map of the area is that of John Rocque in 1757.

Some estate maps of the 18th and 19th centuries; plans of roads and buildings, mainly from 19th and 20th centuries; a small collection of sales catalogues including plans from the later 19th century; maps produced by the constituent local authorities; and geological and land use maps. Goad plans of shopping centres for various areas in the borough, earliest dating from 1969.

Copies of tithe maps for Chipping Barnet and East Barnet, Edgware, Finchley, Friern Barnet, Hendon and Monken Hadley. Enclosure maps of Chipping Barnet and East Barnet 1817 and Finchley 1814.

8.2 Ordnance Survey maps

6 INCHES: 1 MILE (1: 10,560); 1: 10,000 (approx. 6 inches: 1 mile)
1873, 1897, 1920 (incomplete).
1951, 1968 to date (incomplete).

25 INCHES: 1 MILE; 1: 2,500 (approx. 25 inches: 1 mile)
1864, 1896, 1914, 1936 (incomplete).
1951 to date (incomplete).

1: 1,250 (approx. 50 inches: 1 mile)
Current sheets.

9. AUDIO-VISUAL ITEMS

Some films including the Hendon Charter Day 1932; Hendon Show 1954 and 1955; and the Finchley Carnival 1988.

Small collection of videos including *Barnet before doomsday: the early history of a London Borough* 1984, and videos showing the work of various community groups and organisations.

11. LOCAL AUTHORITY RECORDS AND RECORDS OF PREDECESSOR AUTHORITIES

11.1 Barnet Urban District area

CHIPPING BARNET PARISH
Rate assessments 1863-1864.

TOTTERIDGE PARISH
Rate assessments 1792.
Window tax 1790.

BARNET URBAN DISTRICT COUNCIL
Council minutes 1895-1965.
Committee minutes:
 Allotments Committee 1918-1923.
 Civil Defence (War Emergency) Committee 1939-1943, 1949-1951.
 General Purposes Committee 1894-1899.
 Rating and Valuation Committee 1926-1950.
 South Herts Youth Employment Committee 1950-1965.
Rate assessments 1914-1921, 1923-1924, 1934-1956.

11.2 East Barnet Valley Urban District area

EAST BARNET PARISH
Poor Law records:
 Overseers' minutes 1913-1922
 Other records 1866-1927.
Tithe register 1840.

EAST BARNET VALLEY LOCAL BOARD
Board minutes 1875-1894.
Committee minutes:
 Farm Committee reports 1882-1886.
 Lighting Committee 1888-1892.
Medical Officer of Health reports 1891-1894.
Rate assessments 1875-1894.

EAST BARNET VALLEY URBAN SANITARY DISTRICT
Minutes 1870-1874.

EAST BARNET VALLEY URBAN DISTRICT COUNCIL (1895-1935) [later EAST BARNET URBAN DISTRICT COUNCIL (1935-1965)]

Council minutes 1895-1965.
Committee minutes:
>   Allotments Committee 1913-1927.
>   Committees report book 1903-1912.
>   Farm Committee 1913-1927.
>   Finance Committee 1913-1959.
>   Fire Brigade Committee 1913-1945.
>   Food Control Committee 1917-1920.
>   General Purposes Committee 1913-1959.
>   Housing Committee 1913-1927, 1947-1959.
>   Lighting Committee 1924-1934.
>   Miscellaneous Committees 1913-1959.
>   Public Health Committee 1945-1947.
>   Rating and Valuation Committee 1927-1955.
>   Recreation Ground and Baths Committee 1914-1932.
>   Recreation Grounds Committee 1923-1945.
>   Staff Committee 1930-1932.
>   Town Planning Committee 1913-1944, 1951-1964.
>   War Relief Committee 1914-1924.

Medical Officer of Health reports 1895-1964 (gaps).
Rate assessments and other rating records 1895-1959.

11.3 Finchley Borough area

FINCHLEY PARISH

Vestry minutes 1768-1874.
Committee minutes:
>   Sewers Committee 1869-1872.
Highway and paving records:
>   Highway accounts 1851-1852.
>   Surveyors' accounts 1780-1840.
Poor Law records:
>   Settlement examinations 1744-1846.
Sanitary inspector's reports 1889-1893.
Rate assessments 1784-1798, 1816-1834, 1836-1893.
Enclosure award 1817.
Other records 1857-1879.

FINCHLEY LOCAL BOARD

Board minutes 1878-1894.
Committee minutes:
>   Fire Committee 1894-1904.
>   Sanitary Committee 1883-1894.

FINCHLEY SCHOOL BOARD
Board minutes 1881-1903.

FINCHLEY URBAN DISTRICT COUNCIL
Council minutes 1895-1933.
Committee minutes:
     Education Committee 1903-1933.
     Electricity Committee 1906-1913.
     Fire Committee 1894-1904.
     Fire and Water Committee 1904-1923.
     Highway Committee 1897-1914.
     Public Health Committee 1907-1915.
     Recreation Ground Committee 1900-1903.
     Sanitary Committee 1895-1907.
     Town Planning Committee 1914-1915.
     Tramways and Electric Lighting Committee 1901-1906.
     Water Committee 1901-1904.
Medical Officer of Health reports 1928-1933.
Rate assessments 1894-1933.

FINCHLEY BOROUGH COUNCIL
Council minutes 1933-1965.
Committee minutes:
     Education Committee 1933-1965.
Annual accounts 1933-1964.
Medical Officer of Health reports 1934-1938, 1947-1964.
Rate assessments 1933-1961.

11.4 Friern Barnet Urban District area

FRIERN BARNET PARISH
Highway and paving records:
     Highway Surveyors' accounts 1783-1786.
Poor Law records:
     Overseers' minutes 1895-1922.
     Overseers' accounts 1800, 1818, 1836-1870.
Rate assessments 1782, 1794, 1796, 1807, 1815, 1859-1871, 1873-1883.

FRIERN BARNET LOCAL BOARD
Board minutes 1884-1894.

FRIERN BARNET URBAN DISTRICT COUNCIL
Council minutes 1894-1965.
Committee minutes:
     Care Committee 1930-1939.

Education Commitee 1946-1965.
Public Health Committee 1940-1965.
Youth Committee 1947-1959.
Medical Officer of Health reports 1952-1960, 1964.
Rate assessments and other rating records 1914, 1935-1961.

11.5 Hendon Borough area

EDGWARE PARISH
Poor Law records:
Overseers' minutes 1919-1923.
Settlement examinations 1822-1833.
Rate assessments 1853-1871.
Edgwarebury Common tithe award 1845.
Other records 1826.

EDGWARE PARISH COUNCIL
Parish council minutes 1894-1931.
Other records 1895-1898, 1922-1923.

HENDON PARISH
Vestry minutes 1706-1775, 1785-1913.
Draft vestry minutes 1757-1785.
Committee minutes:
Nuisance Removal committee 1856.
Churchwardens' accounts 1656-1893.
Highway and paving records:
Highway surveyors' accounts 1703-1746, 1765-1859.
Poor Law records:
Overseers' accounts 1703-1728, 1743-1837.
Settlement and removal records 1704-1835.
Bastardy records 1727-1834.
Apprenticeship records 1698-1837.
Other records 1785-1858.
Rate assessments 1658-1858, 1872-1874 (Some assessments appear in Churchwardens' accounts,
Overseers' accounts and Highway Surveyors' accounts).
Constables' records 1754-1834.
Census enumerators' returns 1801, 1811, 1821.
Property and endowment records 1596-1855.
Tithe award 1840.

HENDON LOCAL BOARD
Board minutes 1879-1894.

HENDON SANITARY AUTHORITY
Accounts 1879-1885.
Complaints books 1881-1894.
Medical Officer of Health reports 1891-1894.

HENDON SCHOOL BOARD
Board minutes 1898-1903.

HENDON URBAN DISTRICT COUNCIL
Council minutes 1895-1932.
Committee minutes:
>Building Committee 1928-1930.
>Building and Town Planning Committee 1930-1932.
>Education Committee 1903-1932.
>Estates, Parks and Allotments Committee 1928-1932.
>Finance and General Purposes Committee [formerly Finance Committee] 1897-1932.
>Highways Committee 1913-1932.
>Hospital Committee 1913-1915.
>Housing Committee 1920-1921, 1924-1932.
>Joint Medical and Child Welfare Committee 1925-1928.
>Lighting Committee 1899-1903.
>Maternity and Child Welfare Committee 1917-1925.
>Outdoor Committee 1897-1909.
>Public Health Committee 1929-1932.
>Public Libraries Committee 1919-1932.
>Rating and Valuation Committee 1926-1932.
>Sewage Disposal Committee 1913-1928.
>Special Committees 1896-1902.
>Town Planning and Sewerage Committee 1911-1913.
>Works and Fire Brigade Committee 1895-1932.

Medical Officer of Health reports 1895-1932.
Public Health records:
>Complaint books 1895-1911.
>Medical Officer's report books 1910-1916.
>Sanitary Inspector's journal 1918-1931.

Rate assessments 1895-1933.

HENDON BOROUGH
Council minutes 1932-1965.
Committee minutes:
>Appointments Committee 1949-1964.
>Borough Show and Entertainments Committee 1951-1956.
>Civic Restaurants Committee 1947-1950.
>Buildings and Town Planning Committee 1932-1965.
>Civil Defence Committees 1939-1940 (including Air Raid Precautions, Emergency and Civil Defence Committees), 1951-1965.

Education Committee 1932-1965.
Establishment Committee 1949-1965.
Estates, Parks and Allotments Committee 1932-1965.
Finance Committee 1932-1965.
Fire Brigade Committee 1932-1942.
Highways Committee 1932-1942.
Highways and Town Planning Committee 1945-1965.
Housing Committee 1932-1942, 1945-1965.
Libraries and Local Pensions Committee 1935-1939.
Libraries Committee 1945-1957.
Libraries and Museums Committee 1957-1965.
Public Health and Medical Services Committee 1932-1965.
Rating and Valuation Committee 1932-1958.
Town Planning Committee 1932-1938.
Whitley Works Committee 1947-1961.
Works Committee 1932-1942, 1945-1965.
Works and Fire Brigade Committee 1945-1947.
Annual accounts 1933-1964.
Medical Officer of Health reports 1933-1964.
Public Health records:
Sanitary Inspector's journal 1933-1952.
Rate assessments 1933-1958/59.

11.6 London Borough of Barnet

Council minutes 1964 to date.
Committee minutes 1967 to date.

13. RECORDS OF OTHER PUBLIC AUTHORITIES

FINCHLEY CITIZENS ADVICE BUREAU
Minutes 1939-1949.

FRIERN BARNET COUNCIL OF SOCIAL SERVICE
Minutes 1949-1954.

16. RECORDS OF PARISHES

ST BARNABAS HOLDEN ROAD, WOODSIDE PARK [Finchley]
Records 1886-1981.

17. RECORDS OF NON-ANGLICAN PLACES OF WORSHIP

17.1 Non-conformist churches

BALLARDS LANE BAPTIST CHURCH, *Finchley, Middlesex*
Marriage registers 1948-1980.

CHURCH END CONGREGATIONAL CHURCH, *Victoria Avenue, Finchley, Middlesex*
Records 1906-1972.

DARTMOUTH ROAD METHODIST CHAPEL, *West Hendon, Hendon, Middlesex*
Minutes 1934.

EAST FINCHLEY METHODIST CHURCH, *High Road, East Finchley, Finchley, Middlesex*
Records 1867-1994.

EDGWARE CONGREGATIONAL CHURCH, *Grove Road, Edgware, Middlesex*
Registers:
> Baptism 1836-1900.
> Burial 1835-1902.
Church roll 1833-1917.
Other records 1851-1961.

FINCHLEY AND HENDON CIRCUIT
Methodist.
Records 1844-1980.

GOLDERS GREEN METHODIST CHURCH, *Hodford Road, Golders Green, Hendon, Middlesex*
Records 1911-1990.
Includes records of St Ninian's Presbyterian Church, Finchley Road, and Hampstead Wesleyan Methodist Chapel.

HENDON WESLEYAN CHAPEL, *Hendon, Middlesex*
Minutes 1885-1954.

NORTH FINCHLEY CONGREGATIONAL CHURCH, *Nether Street, Finchley, Middlesex*
Baptism registers, marriage registers and church roll 1865-1932.

STATION ROAD BAPTIST CHURCH, *New Barnet, Hertfordshire*
Marriage registers 1911-1979.

UNION CHURCH, *Northiam, Totteridge, Hertfordshire*
Records 1940s-

21. RECORDS OF HOSPITALS, ASYLUMS AND DISPENSARIES

CENTRAL LONDON SICK ASYLUM [later COLINDALE HOSPITAL], *Colindale Avenue, Colindale, Hendon, Middlesex*
Plan and elevations of proposed asylum 1895.

HENDON COTTAGE HOSPITAL, *Hendon Way, Hendon, Middlesex*
Annual reports 1913 to date.

MANOR HOUSE HOSPITAL, *North End Road, Golders Green, Hendon, Middlesex*
Annual reports 1923 to date.

23. RECORDS OF SCHOOLS AND COLLEGES

ALDER SCHOOL, *Long Lane, Finchley, Middlesex*
Admission register 1898-1921.
Log books 1884-1938.

CHRIST'S COLLEGE, *Hendon Lane, Finchley, Middlesex*
Board of Governors' minutes 1906-1911.
General Committee minutes 1902.
School magazine 1926-1941, 1945 to date.
Other records 1849-1942.

FINCHLEY COUNTY SCHOOL, *High Road, Finchley, Middlesex*
Governors' minutes 1909-1919.

HAMPSTEAD GARDEN SUBURB INSTITUTE, *Central Square, Hampstead Garden Suburb, Middlesex*
Deeds 1918-1930.

HENDON CHARITY SCHOOL, *Church Street, Hendon, Middlesex*
Minutes 1787-1913.
Cashbook 1787-1875.
Account of its founding, with list of bequests 1766, 1854.
Sales particulars and plan 1857.

HENDON NATIONAL SCHOOLS, *Church Walk, Hendon, Middlesex*
Minutes 1858-1876.
Cashbooks 1881-1891.

HOLY TRINITY SCHOOL, *East End Road, Finchley, Middlesex*
Minutes 1846-1965.
Admission registers 1871-1953.

Attendance registers 1878-1953.
Log books 1872-1982.

LONG LANE SCHOOL, *Finchley, Middlesex*
Admission register 1898-1921.
Log books 1884-1938.

27. RECORDS OF FIRE AND SALVAGE BRIGADES

HENDON VOLUNTEER FIRE BRIGADE
Records 1860-1873.

28. RECORDS OF MILITARY AND ARMED BODIES

HENDON ASSOCIATION
Minutes 1792-1793.

29. RECORDS OF ASSOCIATIONS, CLUBS AND SOCIETIES

BARNET URBAN DISTRICT RATEPAYERS ASSOCIATION
Minutes 1934-1937.

CHIPPING BARNET CONSERVATIVE ASSOCIATION
Records 1948-1980.

DANIEL AND NICOLL CHARITIES, *Hendon, Middlesex*
Records 1728-1960.

EDGWARE TOWNSWOMEN'S GUILD
Records 1935-1975.

FINCHLEY AND FRIERN BARNET CONSERVATIVE ASSOCIATION
Records 1912-1964.

FINCHLEY MANOR LAWN TENNIS CLUB
Records 1887-1987.

FINCHLEY RATEPAYERS ASSOCIATION
Records 1953 to date.

FINCHLEY ROTARY CLUB
Records 1926-1986.

FINCHLEY TOWNSWOMEN'S GUILD
Minutes 1952-1986.

FRIERN BARNET AND DISTRICT RESIDENTS ASSOCIATION
Records 1931-1998.

FRIERN BARNET TOWNSWOMENS' GUILD
Records 1967-1986.

GOLDERS GREEN PARLIAMENT
Records 1946-1950.

HENDON CO-OPERATIVE POLITICAL COUNCIL
Accounts 1926-1939.

HENDON CRICKET CLUB
Ledger 1852-1892.

HENDON DEBATING SOCIETY
Minutes 1879-1919.
Accounts 1894-1914.
Attendance book 1893-1901.

HENDON HOCKEY CLUB
Records 1909-1982.

HENDON HORTICULTURAL SOCIETY
Records 1909-1954.

HENDON LABOUR PARTY
Records 1924-1987.

HENDON TOWNSWOMEN'S GUILD
Minutes 1939-1979.

HENDON YOUNG MENS FRIENDLY SOCIETY
Records 1893-1897.

HIGHGATE LADIES HOCKEY CLUB
Records 1931-1965.

LONDON CYCLING CAMPAIGN: BARNET GROUP
Records 1983-2000.

MILL HILL THIRTY CLUB
Minutes 1913-1954.

MILL HILL TOWNSWOMEN'S GUILD
Minutes 1951-1982.

SOUTH HENDON LABOUR PARTY
Election files 1990-1994.

SOUTH HENDON LIBERAL DEMOCRATS
Records 1949-1987.

TOTTERIDGE AFTERNOON WOMENS INSTITUTE
Scrapbook 1972-1987.

WATLING COMMUNITY ASSOCIATION
Records c.1925-1980.

WOODHOUSE SCHOOL ASSOCIATION, *Woodhouse Road, Finchley, Middlesex*
Records 1924-1994.

WOODSIDE CLUB
Visitors book 1886-1952.

33. RECORDS OF BUSINESSES

ALSOP, Frank
Cloth merchant.
Account books 1856-1859.

BALAAMS FORGE, *Holcombe Hill, Mill Hill, Hendon, Middlesex*
Accounts 1856-1887.

J. CHILD AND SON, *Hammers Lane, Mill Hill, Hendon, Middlesex*
Sanitary engineer.
Records 1947-1950.

HENDON BREWERY, *The Hyde, Edgware Road, Hendon, Middlesex*
Papers 1897-1914.

35. MANORIAL RECORDS

CHIPPING BARNET
Court minutes 1788.
Admissions and surrenders 1766-1834.
Map 1817.

CLITTERHOUSE, *Hendon,* **Middlesex**
Plan of holding of Kemp Family 1389-1907.

EDGWARE
Grants of manor 1506, 1511, 1522.
Extent 1397.

HENDON
Abstract of charter granted by King Edward the Confessor 1066 with confirmation to 1693.
Court Baron and Court Leet draft minutes 1760-1769.
Rentals 1658, 1709, 1771-1772.
Surveys 1321 (copied 1606), 1574/76, 1632, 1635, 1685/87, 1687, 1754 (copied 1783).
Other records 1771, 1782, 1825, 1829, 1863-1864.

OLD FOLD, *Monken Hadley,* **Middlesex**
Account book of Thomas Allen 1774-1779.

37. ANTIQUARIANS' COLLECTIONS

37.2 Other collections

BANKS, C.O.
Historical notes, transcripts of parish, manorial and other records relating to Finchley and Friern Barnet. Compiled c.1920-1950.

DAVENPORT, Percy
Transcripts of wills for Edgware 1401-1787, Finchley, Friern Barnet, Hendon 1348-1803 and 1831-1838 and Totteridge. Transcripts from records of Middlesex Land Registry for Edgware 1709-1835 and Hendon 1709-1813. Transcripts of Hendon court rolls 1688-1800, officer's accounts 1316-1374 and indentures 1709-1715.

JAMES, N. Brett
Historical notes, transcripts of parish, manorial and other records relating to Hendon and Mill Hill. Manuscript articles, scrapbooks and illustrations. Compiled 1910-1960.

KEMP, F. Hitchin
Notes relating to Hendon and transcript of St Mary Hendon marriage registers 1653-1837.

MILL HILL SOCIETY COLLECTION
Material about the history of Hendon, particularly Mill Hill.

Kingsway Tram Tunnel, Southampton Row, c. 1908

London Borough of Camden

Camden Local Studies and Archives Centre
Holborn Library
32-38 Theobalds Road
London
WC1X 8PA

Tel:
020-7974 6342

Fax:
020-7974 6284

E-mail:
localstudies@camden.gov.uk

Website:
www.camden.gov.uk/localstudies

Location:
On second floor of Holborn Library.
Lifts. Disabled access except to meetings room.

Nearest stations:
Chancery Lane (Central Line) 450 metres, Farringdon (Circle Line, Hammersmith and City Line, Metropolitan Line, Thameslink) 750 metres, Holborn (Central and Piccadilly Lines), 550 metres.

Parking:
Limited metered street parking. Car parks in Brunswick Square and Saffron Hill. Single disabled parking space in John's Mews, immediately behind Holborn Library.

Days of opening:
Monday, Tuesday, Thursday, Friday, Saturday.
Appointments only required to see archives from out-store (J).

Administrative history:
The London Borough of Camden comprises the former Metropolitan Boroughs of Hampstead, Holborn and St Pancras. All were in the County of Middlesex before 1889 and in the County of London 1889-1965.

The ancient parishes in the area were Hampstead, St Andrew Holborn (part of which lay in the City of London), St Giles in the Fields and St Pancras. St Andrew Holborn above Bars (i.e. the part outside the City of London) and St Giles in the Fields were divided in the 18th century to create the parishes of St George the Martyr Queen Square and St George Bloomsbury respectively. The eastern part of the parish of St Andrew Holborn formed the Liberty of Saffron Hill, Hatton Garden, Ely Place and Ely Rents.

Two boards of works were created in 1855. The St Giles District Board covered the parishes of St Giles in the Fields and St George Bloomsbury. The Holborn District Board covered the parishes of St Andrew Holborn above Bars, St George the Martyr Queen Square, St Sepulchre Middlesex and the Liberty of Glasshouse Yard (The last two are now in the London Borough of Islington). After 1855 the parishes of Hampstead and St Pancras assumed extra responsibilities. The records of these two vestries are described separately.

The Holborn Poor Law Union covered the parishes of St Andrew Holborn above Bars and St George the Martyr Queen Square, and the Liberty of Saffron Hill. The St Giles in the Fields and St George Bloomsbury Board of Guardians covered the parishes of St Giles in the Fields and St George Bloomsbury; it became part of the Holborn Union in 1914. The Hampstead Board of Guardians was formed under a local act of Parliament in 1801 and was part of the Edmonton Union 1837-1848. The Directors of the Poor for St Pancras resisted the formation of a Board of Guardians throughout much of the 19th century but eventually a St Pancras Board of Guardians was established in 1867.

Holdings:
The Local Studies Section was created in 1974. Its holdings are based upon the former Hampstead, Holborn and St Pancras local history collections. The section moved to a new Centre on the 2nd floor of Holborn Library in 1995. Many archives are held in an out-store (J) behind Holborn Library. The total number of items held is estimated to be over 175,000.

Catalogues and indexes:
Card catalogues, arranged by author, title and subject for books, maps and other printed material.
Card catalogues for illustrations, arranged by subject and artist, engraver etc.
General Index 1967 to date: Local information. Indexes deeds, letters and other documents, as well as local newspapers and council and committee agendas until 1978.
Lists of parish, local authority and some deposited archives.
Separate catalogues for the former Hampstead, Holborn and St Pancras collections.
Computer catalogue in progress.

Research guides:
ASTON, Mark, KNIGHT, Richard and HOLMES, Malcolm, *Camden past and present: a guide to the Camden Local Studies and Archives Centre* (2000).
Free information sheets on various subjects including parish registers, tracing the history of a building and family history and genealogy.

Postal, telephone and e-mail enquiries:
Information about the Centre supplied on request. Although staff are unable to carry out research, a list of researchers can be supplied. Answering machine for messages when the Centre is closed.

Services:

Photographic service; reproduction fees may be charged.

Photocopying facilities; original and fragile material may not be copied; copyright restrictions apply to some items.

Microfilm/fiche reader/printer.

Free Internet access to local history and family history websites.

Small loan collection of older duplicate books.

Slide loan collection.

Regular exhibitions on local history.

Talks; fees usually charged; tours of the Centre for groups.

Publications on sale; postal service; order form available.

Related collections held elsewhere:

BURGH HOUSE
New End Square
London
NW3 1LT
(tel: 020-7435 0144)
Contains the Hampstead Museum of Local History. Art exhibitions, lectures and other events. Friends newsletter.

HIGHGATE LITERARY AND SCIENTIFIC INSTITUTION
11 South Grove
London
N6 6BS
(tel: 020-8340 3343)
Extensive collection on the history of Highgate.

KEATS HOUSE
Keats Grove
London
NW3 2RR
(tel: 020-7435 2062)
Museum relating to John Keats and the Romantic Movement.

1. BOOKS, PAMPHLETS AND PERIODICALS

Books including histories of areas in the borough, immediately adjacent areas and general books on London. Biographies of people who have lived in the borough where there are strong local connections. Large collections of books, periodicals and other materials on George Bernard Shaw and Charles Dickens. Material about 'national' bodies with their headquarters in Camden and items published 'locally' are not normally collected.

Many small pamphlets, articles from journals and items of ephemera.

Several hundred periodical titles including newsletters from churches, community and residents' groups, local societies, schools and hospitals. Historical and archaeological periodicals relating to London and about local history, family history and archives. Most local periodicals are for recent years only but a number of 19th century parish magazines are held.

Victoria County History:
Middlesex vol. 9 – Hampstead.

Selected books on other areas:
CAMDEN HISTORY SOCIETY. *Streets of series*. Volumes include East of Bloomsbury, Bloomsbury and Fitzrovia, Old Holborn, Primrose Hill to Euston Road, St Giles in the Fields and St Pancras.
RICHARDSON, John. *Highgate: its history since the fifteenth century* (1983).
RICHARDSON, John. *Kentish Town past* (1997).

2. SPECIAL COLLECTIONS OF PRINTED MATERIAL

BEATTIE COLLECTION
Works of William Beattie M.D. (1793-1875), a Hampstead doctor, including memoirs, travel books and poems. About 200 items including books and manuscripts. Acquired by Professor Henry Morley. *Separate catalogue.*

ELEANOR FARJEON COLLECTION
Books by and about Hampstead author Eleanor Farjeon. Presented by the author in 1960. Additional items have been added to collection. *Separate catalogue.*

HUGHES BEQUEST
About 860 items by and about George Bernard Shaw including books, cuttings, photographs, ephemera and recordings.

KATE GREENAWAY COLLECTION
Books, proofs, greetings cards and some original drawings. Presented by the artist's brother. Additional items have been added to collection. *Separate catalogue. Available by appointment only.*

For details of special collections of illustrations see pp.43-44, for details of Sharpe Collection see p.46; for details of antiquarians' collections see p.68.

3. NEWSPAPERS

No photocopying from bound volumes. Newspapers in fragile condition may not be available for use. In the 1960s and 1970s some local newspapers were indexed in the General Index (see p.34). Since 1978 many newspapers have been scanned and press cut (see p.38).

NEW VESTRYMAN AND METROPOLITAN PAROCHIAL GAZETTE 1833-1834.

METROPOLITAN 1856-1857, 1875.

UNITED ALBION GAZETTE 1866; continued as CAMDEN AND KENTISH TOWNS GAZETTE 1866-1919; continued as ST PANCRAS GAZETTE 1919-1939.
Incorporated with Islington and Holloway Press 1939.

NORTH LONDONER 1870-1874; continued as ST PANCRAS AND HOLBORN GUARDIAN 1875.
Continued from June 1875 as two newspapers, St Pancras Guardian and Holborn Guardian.

HAMPSTEAD AND HIGHGATE EXPRESS 1872-1874 (gaps), 1875 to date.
E.F. Oppe's index 1890-1951 (very selective).

KILBURN TIMES 1872-1874, 1876-1878, 1880-1887, 1893, 1923-1925, 1927, 1928, 1945-1950, 1952, 1956-1967, 1969 to date.

ST PANCRAS GUARDIAN 1875-1898.

SOUTH HAMPSTEAD ADVERTISER 1882-1883; continued as ST JOHN'S WOOD AND SOUTH HAMPSTEAD ADVERTISER 1883-1890; continued as ST JOHN'S WOOD, KILBURN AND HAMPSTEAD ADVERTISER 1890-1906; continued as HAMPSTEAD AND ST JOHN'S WOOD ADVERTISER 1906-1913; continued as HAMPSTEAD, ST JOHN'S WOOD AND KILBURN ADVERTISER 1913-1936; continued as HAMPSTEAD NEWS 1936-1971.

HAMPSTEAD RECORD 1889-1918; continued as HAMPSTEAD AND HIGHGATE RECORD 1918-1938, 1950-1966.

HOLBORN AND FINSBURY GUARDIAN 1893, 1894, 1899-1928, 1931-1963; continued as CAMDEN AND HOLBORN AND FINSBURY GUARDIAN 1963-1980; continued as HOLBORN AND CITY GUARDIAN 1980-1989.

ST PANCRAS CHRONICLE 1928-1930 (gaps), 1932-1937 (gaps), 1939-1950 (gaps) 1951-1963; continued as CAMDEN AND ST PANCRAS CHRONICLE 1963-1997; continued as CAMDEN CHRONICLE 1997 to date.

PEOPLE'S ADVERTISER 1936, 1953-1966.

ISLINGTON AND HOLLOWAY PRESS 1941-1942 (gaps).

NORTH LONDON PRESS 1943-1951 (gaps), 1952-1971.
Camden Edition. Continued as Camden Journal.

CAMDEN JOURNAL 1971-1980.

SAVE THE JOURNAL 1981.
Produced by striking journalists from Camden Journal.

HAMPSTEAD GUARDIAN 1981.

CAMDEN NEW JOURNAL 1982 to date.

HAMPSTEAD AND DISTRICT LOCAL ADVERTISER 1982-1985; continued as HAMPSTEAD LOCAL ADVERTISER 1985; continued as HAMPSTEAD ADVERTISER 1985-1993 (gaps).

COVENT GUARDIAN 1982-1985 (gaps).

HAMPSTEAD POST 1988-1989 (gaps).

4. CUTTINGS COLLECTIONS

Volumes of newscuttings before 1957 relating to Hampstead, covering subjects such as murders, library events and local organisations. Other newscuttings particularly for 1950s–1970s in Hampstead, Holborn and St Pancras collections. Microfiche of cuttings from local and national newspapers 1978 to date. Newscuttings from Camden Council Public Relations section 1990-1994.

The Heal Collection (see p.68) contains cuttings about St Pancras from 18th, 19th and early 20th centuries. The Bellmoor Collection (see p.68) has 19th and early 20th century cuttings for Hampstead.

5. DIRECTORIES

5.1 Court guides

ABC COURT GUIDE AND FASHIONABLE YEARBOOK
1871.

BOYLE'S COURT GUIDE
1808, 1820, 1829, 1834, 1840, 1842-1846, 1879, 1882, 1883, 1887, 1893, 1894, 1898, 1904, 1908, 1923.

THE ROYAL BLUE BOOK
1858.

WEBSTER'S ROYAL BLUE BOOK
1906, 1915.

5.2 London, county and general directories

ESSEX, HERTS AND MIDDLESEX
Kelly's.
1937.

LONDON
Little London.
1677 (1878 reprint).

LONDON
Microfilm of various directories.
1749-1760, 1779-1781, 1795-1797, 1800-1805.

LONDON
J. Payne.
1769.

LONDON
Post Office (Various publishers until 1836; from 1837 Kelly's).
1800-1991 (gaps).

LONDON
Holden's Triennial.
1805/07.

LONDON
Kent's.
1813.

LONDON INCLUDING MIDDLESEX AND SOUTHERN COUNTIES
Pigot and Co. London and Provincial New Commercial.
1823/24.

LONDON
Robson's.
1832.

LONDON INCLUDING EASTERN COUNTIES
Pigot and Co. Royal National and Commercial.
1839.

LONDON
Robson's Commercial.
1840.

LONDON
Kelly's Northern Suburbs.
1872.

MIDDLESEX
Kelly's.
1933, 1937.

5.3 Local directories

BARNET AND EAST BARNET
Borough Directories Ltd (London Borough of Barnet Directory vol. 3).
1969.

CAMDEN TOWN AND KENTISH TOWN
Hutchings and Crowsley to 1885/86; later editions Kelly's.
1867, 1874, 1884/85, 1904, 1907-1910, 1911/12-1914/15, 1922, 1923, 1926/27.

FINCHLEY
Borough Directories Ltd (London Borough of Barnet Directory vol. 2).
1970.

HAMPSTEAD
J.J. Shaw.
1854.

HAMPSTEAD AND HIGHGATE
'Express' G.S. Jealous.
1873.

HAMPSTEAD AND HIGHGATE
Hutchings and Crowsley to 1886/87; later editions Kelly's.
1873, 1885/86, 1888/89, 1894/95, 1896-1901, 1903-1940.

HAMPSTEAD
Provost and Co.; later editions Hampstead Press; Baines and Scarbrook. (Hampstead Yearbook).
1888-1908.

HAMPSTEAD
Baines and Scarsbrook Ltd (Local Guide and Almanack).
1896-1914.

HAMPSTEAD
Baines and Scarsbrook Ltd (Blue Book).
1928-1939.

HAMPSTEAD
London and Provincial Publications Ltd; later Borough Directories Ltd (From 1964 published as London Borough of Camden Directory vol. 1).
1951/52, 1954/55, 1959/60, 1961, 1962/63-1967/68, 1969, 1970.

HENDON
Kelly's.
1926, 1937, 1939.

HENDON
London and Provincial Publications Ltd; later Borough Directories Ltd (From 1964 published as London Borough of Barnet Directory vol. 1).
1950/51–1970/71 (gaps).

HORNSEY
Kelly's.
1938.

KILBURN INCLUDING WILLESDEN, CRICKLEWOOD AND WEST HAMPSTEAD
Kelly's.
1896, 1920, 1921, 1925, 1931-1940.

ST MARYLEBONE
Kelly's.
1938.

ST PANCRAS
James Giddings.
1862.

ST PANCRAS
Simpson's.
1862.

ST PANCRAS INCLUDING HAMPSTEAD AND HIGHGATE
W. Hogg and Co. Ltd.
1864.

ST PANCRAS
Penfold and Farmer (Almanack and Parish Guide).
1882/84.

ST PANCRAS
Borough Directories.
1963/64-1965/66.

5.4 Telephone directories

5.4.1 Central London

LONDON POSTAL AREA, LONDON CENTRAL, LONDON WEST
Residential and Business/Services.
1954-1955 (gaps), 1968 to date (gaps).

5.4.2. Local areas

BARNET
1978, 1980.

5.4.3 Yellow pages

LONDON CENTRAL
1969 to date (gaps).

LONDON NORTH
1972-1994/95 (gaps).

LONDON NORTH-WEST
1977, 1986, 1991/92, 1995/96.

5.4.4 Commercial directories

GREATER LONDON BUSINESS
1969, 1970, 1972.

LONDON BUSINESS PAGES
1985, 1987, 1991, 1992.

LONDON INDUSTRIAL AND COMMERCIAL CLASSIFIED
1971-1973, 1975, 1978, 1981, 1983, 1984.

6. ELECTORAL REGISTERS

HAMPSTEAD
1899-1963.

ST GILES IN THE FIELDS AND ST GEORGE BLOOMSBURY PARISHES [FINSBURY PARLIAMENTARY BOROUGH]
1837.

HOLBORN DIVISION [FINSBURY PARLIAMENTARY BOROUGH]
1878, 1893-1914.

HOLBORN
1918-1963.

ST PANCRAS
1863/64 (County Voters only).

ST PANCRAS [including ST MARYLEBONE]
1866-1871, 1873-1877, 1879-1885.

ST PANCRAS
1886-1897, 1899-1963.

LONDON BOROUGH OF CAMDEN
1964 to date.

7. ILLUSTRATIONS

About 50,000 illustrations. Illustration indexes include entries for pictures in other sources, for example books.

Prints, drawings, watercolours and some oil paintings, mostly 19th century, including original works by Frederick Adcock, J.P. Emslie, Geoffrey S. Fletcher, S.H. Grimm, F.J. Sarjeant, Sidney Arrobus and Thomas Hosmer Shepherd. Index to artists, engravers etc. The Kentish Town Rolls, a series of 19th century pen and ink drawings, by James Frederick King depict scenes on the road from St Pancras Old Church to Highgate Road (published by the Centre as the *Kentish Town Panorama*).

Photographs from 1860s but most date from 1890s-1920s, 1940-1945 and 1950s to date. Photographs 1903-1904 of every building above the Northern and Piccadilly Underground lines within the borough. Civil Defence photographs 1940-1945 of most bomb sites within the former Borough of Holborn. Photographs of many council buildings 1960s-1980s. Aerial photographs. Some glass negatives.

Slide Collection containing many reproductions of material in the Centre, together with modern scenes. Most available for loan.

Special collections:

ANTHONY COOPER BEQUEST
Photographs following the route of the Regent's Canal in Camden. Taken in 1994.

CAMDEN HISTORY SOCIETY PHOTOGRAPHIC SURVEY

Photographic survey of the borough, initiated by the Camden History Society in 1973. The following areas in Holborn and St Pancras have been systematically photographed: Camden Town (part), Chalk Farm, Covent Garden (Camden part only), Fitzrovia, Hatton Garden and Saffron Hill area, Highgate New Town, Kentish Town (part), and Tolmers Village.

'CATCHING THE PAST' PHOTOGRAPHIC SURVEY

Photographic survey of all streets in the Borough. Taken in 2000. Organised by the Camden History Society as part of Camden's Millennium History Project.

DALZIEL COLLECTION

Over 250 proof copies of 19th century engravings by the Dalziel brothers (formerly of Hampstead and Camden Town).

HAMPSTEAD AREA CONSERVATION COMMITTEE

Photographs of Hampstead. Taken in the 1970s.

WALLIS COLLECTION

Prints and drawings of Camden and parts of Islington and St Marylebone. Donated by Cyril Wallis.

For details of the Kate Greenaway Collection see p.36; for details of Sharpe Collection see p.46.

8. MAPS

8.1 General maps

Reproductions of London maps from 16th century including William Morgan's London 1682, John Rocque's plan of the Cities of London, Westminster and Southwark 1746 and John Horwood's plan of London and Westminster 1792-1799. Parish and borough maps from 18th century. Approximately 3,000 sheets.

Goad insurance plans 1886-1960 covering many commercial and shopping areas of Camden. Goad plans of shopping streets 1980 to date. Facsimile copies of bomb damage maps covering Camden area produced by the London County Council Architect's Department using 25 inches: 1 mile Ordnance Survey maps. Sale catalogue plans and architectural drawings.

Official maps and plans forming part of local government archives are listed on p.p.46-56, those forming part of estate records on p.65 and other manuscript plans on p.67.

Maps of Hampstead include Belsize Manor 1679, Hampstead Parish Trigometric Survey 1680, J. Ellis' map of Hampstead Manor 1762 with field book (copy of original in London Metropolitan Archives), J. Newton's map of Hampstead 1814 and Hampstead parish tithe map 1839 (copy).

Maps of Holborn include St Andrew Holborn c.1720, 1755, St Giles in the Fields c.1720, 1755 and

C.J.J. Mair's map of St Giles in the Fields and St George Bloomsbury 1866.

Maps of St Pancras include Cantelowes Demesne Lands Parliamentary survey 1649 (copy) and parish maps for 1801, 1804 (with terrier book), 1834, 1849, 1860, 1868, 1874, 1880, 1893.

8.2 Ordnance Survey maps

6 INCHES: 1 MILE (1: 10,560); 1: 10,000 (approx. 6 inches: 1 mile)
1862-1873, 1893-1895, 1911-1914, 1938, 1951 to date (incomplete).

12 INCHES: 1 MILE (1: 5,280)
1848-1851. Camden Town, Euston and Holborn. Skeleton survey.

25 INCHES: 1 MILE; 1: 2,500 (approx. 25 inches 1 mile)
1865-1874, 1891-1894, 1910s-1920s, 1930s, 1951 to date (incomplete).

60 INCHES: 1 MILE (1: 1,056)
1848-1851. Hampstead Heath and Highgate. Skeleton Survey.
1865-1874, 1891-1894, 1910s-1920s, 1930s (incomplete).

1: 1,250 (approx. 50 inches: 1 mile)
1951 to date (gaps).

ADMINISTRATIVE MAPS (1: 25,000 and 1: 63,360)
1947 to date. Camden and Greater London areas.

9. AUDIO-VISUAL ITEMS

Small collection of films and videos. Videos may be viewed at the Centre by appointment.

Films include: one of St Pancras Council in session; air raid precautions in the Second World War; and others about the Borough of Hampstead, including *About Hampstead* 1950s.

Videos include: *Epitaph for an age* 1974, about Highgate Cemetery; *Tolmers Square: beginning or end?* 1975, a BBC Community Unit programme; *What do I remember now?* 1985, describing Queen's Crescent Market, Kentish Town; *Arrobus '88* 1988, a film of an exhibition about Hampstead artist Sidney Arrobus; and the *British Library at St Pancras* 1991. Other videos include ones produced by Camden Council promoting and publicising local services during the 1980s and 1990s.

Some reel-to-reel tape recordings, including the opening of Swiss Cottage Library 1964, and Holborn Library 1960. Gramophone records include George Bernard Shaw's acceptance of the Freedom of the Metropolitan Borough of St Pancras, 9 October 1946, and other recordings of his works.

Tape recordings of the Camden Oral History Project 1986-1987 and transcripts, where available.

10. COLLECTIONS OF MUSEUM OBJECTS

SHARPE COLLECTION
Collection of 19th century family toys, books, pressed flowers, Christmas and Valentine cards, photographs etc. of Elizabeth Sharpe of Admiral's House, Hampstead 1865-1905.

11. LOCAL AUTHORITY RECORDS AND RECORDS OF PREDECESSOR AUTHORITIES

DISTRICT JOINT BOARD (AREA 10) GREATER LONDON
Employers and employees joint negotiating board for local government officers.
Minutes 1922-1929 (J).
[Part of the archives of the Metropolitan Borough of St Pancras]

11.1 Hampstead Metropolitan Borough area

HAMPSTEAD PARISH
Vestry minutes 1746-1873.
Assessment Committee 1837-1838.
Churchwardens' accounts [St John Hampstead] 1773-1804 (including abstract of title deeds 1643-1785), 1842-1895.
Highway and paving records:
      Lighting Commissioners' minutes 1775-1855.
      Highway Surveyor's accounts 1767-1845 (J).
      Boundary stones particulars 1854.
      Other records 1792-1793, 1795-1826, 1831-1855.
Poor Law records:
      Guardians' minutes 1800-1816, 1826-1900.
      Overseers' accounts 1826-1837.
      Settlement examinations 1804-1814.
      Workhouse accounts 1734-1739.
      Workhouse visitors' meetings 1809-1813.
      Guardians of the Poor bills 1830-1874.
      [The Hampstead Board of Guardians was created in 1800, but from 1837 until 1848 was absorbed into the Edmonton Union. In 1848 it regained its independent status. Main archive including Guardians' minutes 1817-1825 held at London Metropolitan Archives, 40 Northampton Road, London EC1R 0HB]
Rate assessments and valuation lists 1774, 1777, 1779-1826, 1829-1855.
Census returns: heads of households 1801, 1811.
Other records 1827-1848.

HAMPSTEAD VESTRY
After the Metropolis Local Management Act (1855) additional powers were given to Hampstead Vestry.
Vestry minutes 1855-1900.
Committee minutes:
>   Baths and Wash Houses Committee 1895-1900 (J).
>   Burial Committee 1895-1900 (J).
>   Cleansing, Repairing and Watering Committee 1856-1861 (J).
>   Finance Committee 1879-1900 (J).
>   General Purposes Committee 1895-1900 (J).
>   Highways Committee 1885-1895 (J).
>   Lighting Committee 1892-1900 (J).
>   Public Libraries Committee 1895-1900 (J).
>   Sanitary Committee 1885-1895 (J).
>   Tree and Open Spaces Committee 1885-1900 (J).
>   Works Committee 1879-1900 (J).
>   Other committees 1861-1900 (J).

Annual reports 1856-1900.
Lists of vestrymen and committees [Diaries] 1882/83, 1895/96-1898/99.
Surveyor's reports 1856-1882 (J).
Churchwardens' and overseers' minutes 1868-1900.
Churchwardens' and overseers' accounts 1856-1872, 1874-1901.
Public health records:
>   Sanitary experience of C.J. Lord 1827-1889.

Rate assessments and valuation lists 1856-1900.
Other records 1856-1900.

HAMPSTEAD BATHS AND WASH HOUSES COMMISSIONERS
Minutes 1883-1895 (J).
Other records 1886-1901 (J).

HAMPSTEAD BURIAL BOARD
Minutes 1873-1895 (J).
Register of mortgages 1874-1894 (J).

HAMPSTEAD PUBLIC LIBRARIES AND MUSEUMS COMMISSIONERS
Minutes 1893-1895 (J).
Committee minutes 1893-1895 (J).

HAMPSTEAD METROPOLITAN BOROUGH
Council minutes 1900-1965.
Committee minutes:
>   Air Raid Precautions Committee 1938-1941 (J).
>   Allotments Committee 1921-1927 (J).
>   Assessment Committee 1900-1950 (J).
>   Baths and Wash Houses Committee 1900-1965 (J).

Cemeteries Committee 1900-1937 (J).
Civic Centre Committee 1958-1963 (J).
Civil Defence Committee 1939-1945, 1951-1965 (J).
Distress Committee 1905-1928 (J).
Electricity and Lighting Committee 1900-1948 (J).
Entertainments Committee 1948-1949, 1951-1965 (J).
Establishment Committee 1925-1965 (J). *Closed until 50 years old.*
Finance and General Business Committee 1939-1943 (J).
Finance Committee 1900-1965 (J).
Food Control and Local Distribution Committee 1917-1920 (J).
General Emergency Committee 1939-1944 (J).
General Purposes Committee [formerly Parliamentary and General Purposes Committee] 1900-1965 (J).
Housing Committee 1901-1965 (J).
Libraries Committee 1900-1965 (J).
Maternity and Child Welfare Committee 1919-1948 (J).
Planning Committee 1943-1965 (J).
Public Health Committee 1908-1965 (J).
Road Safety Committee [formerly Hampstead Children's Safety Committee] 1937-1938, 1946-1965 (J).
Tree, Open Spaces (and Cemeteries) Committee 1900-1965 (J).
Works Committee 1900-1965 (J).
Other committees 1900-1965 (J).
Annual reports 1900/01-1911/12, 1929/30-1956/57.
Annual abstract of accounts 1900/01-1962/63.
General rate estimates 1964/65.
Lists of Council and its Committees 1922-1939, 1944, 1946-1954/55, 1957/58-1964/65.
Electric Lighting Department statement of accounts 1903/04, 1910/11-1938/39.
Medical Officer of Health reports 1902-1964.
Public Libraries annual reports 1950/51-1963/64.
Cemetery records:
Fortune Green Cemetery [Hampstead Cemetery] graves in perpetuity 1923-1953 (J).
Civil Defence records:
Damaged property list 1939-1945 (streets A-L only).
Hampstead Civil Defence members register 1938-1940s (J).
Incidents list 1941-1943.
Civil Defence files and papers 1940s (J).
Register of hired premises 1939-1945 (J).
Engineer and Surveyor's Department:
Borough Engineer's files and other papers 1940s-1960s (J).
London County Council plans deposited under the London Building Acts 1902-1934 (J).
Town Clerk's Department:
Distress Committee registers 1908/09-1914/15 (J).
District Food Office files 1917-1918, 1920s (J).
Housing files and papers 1940s–1950s (J).

Papers relating to various subjects including the Great Central Railway extension to London 1891 and Hampstead Electric Lighting 1890s (J).
Rate assessments and valuation lists 1900-1964/65 (J).

11.2 Holborn Metropolitan Borough area

ST ANDREW HOLBORN ABOVE BARS AND ST GEORGE THE MARTYR QUEEN SQUARE VESTRY
Civil parish created in 1767, responsible for the part of the ancient parish of St Andrew Holborn which lay outside the City of London, but excluding the Liberty of Saffron Hill.
General meeting minutes 1812-1900.
Committee minutes 1865-1900.
Highway, paving and watching records:
      Paving Commissioners' annual statements and accounts 1833-1855.
      Paving Commissioners' minutes 1771-1774, 1781-1855.
      Watch Committee minutes 1805-1810.
      Watch Committee reports 1818-1824.
      Other records 1786-1860.
Poor Law records:
      Overseers' special session minutes 1731-1736.
      Overseers' and Churchwardens' weekly meeting minutes 1737-1738.
      Overseers' accounts and disbursements 1785-1798.
      Governors' and Directors' weekly meetings minutes 1812-1816, 1822-1826, 1830-1841, 1847-1850, 1854-1860, 1865-1871, 1878-1900.
      Bastardy examinations 1784-1790.
      Payments to women who nurse their own children 1791-1792, 1796-1799.
      Workhouse admissions and discharges 1750-1759.
      Payments to casual poor in the workhouse 1785-1786, 1798.
      Other records 1736-1745, 1801-1802, 1805-1812, 1825-1835, 1837-1838.
Rate assessments and valuation lists 1729-1732, 1734, 1739-1740, 1742-1760, 1762-1764, 1766-1768, 1771-1778, 1780-1900.
Other records 1762, 1773-1785, 1792-1836, 1842-1900.
[Records for the part of the parish lying within the City of London including the registers of St Andrew Holborn are held at Guildhall Library, Aldermanbury, London EC2P 2EJ]

LIBERTY OF SAFFRON HILL, HATTON GARDEN AND ELY PLACE
Liberty within the parish of St Andrew Holborn consisting of the part that lay east of Leather Lane and north of Holborn.
Minutes and accounts 1659-1777.
General meeting minutes 1816-1832, 1859-1900.
Highway, paving and watching records:
      Paving minutes 1771-1792, 1814-1829, 1855.
      Watch committee minutes 1773-1805.
      Watch committee report book 1817.

Poor Law records:

    Examination book [deserted wives] 1847-1857.

    Pauper examinations 1862-1866.

    Settlement examination books 1775-1785, 1793-1799, 1806-1807, 1810-1812.

    Workhouse accounts 1804-1837 (gaps).

Rate assessments and valuation lists 1726, 1729, 1733, 1736-1900.

Other records 1801-1817, 1827-1837, 1856-1901.

ST GILES IN THE FIELDS PARISH

Vestry minutes 1618-1900.

Committee minutes 1771-1813, 1830-1900.

Churchwardens' and overseers' accounts 1640-1723.

Parish accounts 1680-1681.

Highway, paving and watching records:

    New Paving Committee minutes 1772-1829.

    Highway Repair Committee minutes 1834-1844.

    Other records 1772-1793.

Poor Law records:

    Poor accounts and disbursements 1680-1681, 1699, 1703.

    Register of parish apprentices 1780-1802.

Burial Ground [new ground in Pancras Road] Trustees minutes and accounts 1803-1861.

Cemetery register [new ground in Pancras Road] 1844-1858.

Church rebuilding fund contributors list 1623.

Other records 1805-1900.

ST GEORGE BLOOMSBURY PARISH

Parish created in 1731. Formerly part of the parish of St Giles in the Fields.

Vestry minutes 1731-1900.

Committee minutes 1830-1900.

Churchwardens' and overseers' minutes 1832-1874.

Churchwardens' accounts 1731-1831, 1883-1895.

Committee for care and repair of church and burial ground minutes 1830-1872.

Highway, paving and watching records:

    New Paving Committee minutes 1771-1822.

    Other records 1772-1793, 1818-1822.

Other records 1822-1900.

ST GILES IN THE FIELDS AND ST GEORGE BLOOMSBURY JOINT VESTRY

Joint vestry created by Act of Parliament to deal with civil matters; the parishes of St Giles in the Fields and St George Bloomsbury remained separate for ecclesiastical purposes.

Vestry minutes 1767-1900.

Committee minutes 1830-1900.

Annual reports 1870-1874, 1885-1900.

Highway, paving and watching records:

    Paving Committee minutes 1784-1855.

    Surveyors' Committee minutes 1846-1850.

Watch report 1799-1802.
Other records 1771-1855.
Poor Law records:
    Directors of the Poor minutes 1830-1868.
    Poor abstract account 1822/23-1899/1900.
    Receipts and disbursements 1822-1892.
    Board of accounts minutes [of workhouse] 1830-1868.
    Other records 1775-1864.
Rate assessments and valuation lists 1730-1900.
Other records 1792, 1823-1900.

HOLBORN DISTRICT BOARD OF WORKS
Board of Works covering the parishes of St Andrew Holborn above Bars, St George the Martyr Queen Square and St Sepulchre Middlesex and the Liberties of Saffron Hill and Glasshouse Yard.
Board minutes 1855-1900.
Committee minutes:
    Law and Parliamentary Committee 1893-1900.
    Sanitary Committee 1895-1900.
Annual reports 1856/57-1873/74, 1898/99-1899/1900.
Public health records 1856-1857, 1866-1871, 1895-1897, 1899.
Other records 1856-1901.

ST GILES DISTRICT BOARD OF WORKS
Board covering the parishes of St Giles in the Fields and St George Bloomsbury.
Board minutes 1856-1860, 1866-1900.
Committee minutes:
    Finance Committee 1880-1900.
    Law and Parliamentary Committee 1884-1900.
    Sanitary Committee 1883-1898.
    Works Committee 1856-1900.
    Special Committees 1892-1900.
Annual reports 1856-1900.
Public health records 1878-1883, 1889-1900.
Boundary stones 1877.
Other records 1859-1901.

ST GILES BATHS COMMISSIONERS
Minutes 1850-1854, 1863-1870, 1890-1897.
Other records 1850-1900.

HOLBORN LIBRARY COMMISSIONERS
Annual reports 1891-1900.
Other records 1891-1900.

ST GILES LIBRARIES COMMISSIONERS
Minutes 1891-1899.
Annual reports 1893/94-1899/1900.
Other records 1892-1900.

HOLBORN METROPOLITAN BOROUGH
Council minutes 1900-1965.
Committee minutes:
    Baths Committee 1961-1964 (J).
    Highway and Works Committee 1957-1963 (J).
    Housing and Planning Committee 1962-1965 (J).
    Housing Estates Management Committee 1949-1965 (J). *Closed until 50 years old.*
    Law and Parliamentary Committee 1956-1965 (J).
    Library Committee 1961-1965 (J).
    Public Health Committee 1964-1965 (J).
Annual reports 1900/01-1914/15, 1929/30-1937/38.
Annual estimates 1901-1925.
Yearbooks 1907/08-1911/12, 1914/15-1916, 1919-1941, 1943-1945, 1947-1948, 1950-1964/65.
Abstract of accounts 1905-1930/31, 1947/48-1963/64.
Libraries Committee annual reports 1946/47-1963/64.
Medical Officer of Health reports 1911-1964.
Civil Defence records:
    Air raid incidents record 1940-1945 (J).
    Control room register of unexploded bombs etc. 1940-1945 (J).
Engineer and Surveyor's Department:
    Endell Street Baths rebuilding papers 1930-1931.
    Holborn Town Hall specifications c.1906.
Mayor's Office:
    Charities records 1900-1965 (J).
Treasurer's Department:
    Records 1906-1962/63.
Rate assessments and valuation lists 1900-1934/35; 1935/36-1952/53 (J).

11.3 St Pancras Metropolitan Borough area

ST PANCRAS PARISH
Vestry minutes 1718-1855. *Subject and name indexes and transcripts of extracts.*
Poor Law records:
    Directors of the Poor minutes 1804-1877, 1888-1901 (J).
    Surgeon's report book 1830-1833 (J).
Rate assessments and valuation lists 1801, 1803-1834, 1836-1855.

ST PANCRAS VESTRY
After the Metropolis Local Management Act (1855) additional powers were given to St Pancras Vestry.
Vestry minutes 1855-1900. *Subject and name indexes and transcripts of extracts 1855-1889.*
Committee minutes:
>   Assessment Committee 1870-1871 (J).
>   Finance Committee 1870-1873, 1899-1900 (J).
>   General Purposes Committee 1856-1887, 1889-1900 (J).
>   Health Committee 1856-1900 (J).
>   Highway, Sewers and Public Works Committee 1856-1857, 1859-1900 (J).
Annual reports and accounts 1890/91-1899/1900.
Annual abstracts of accounts 1856-1877, 1882-1892.
Diary and almanac 1895/96,1896/97, 1898/99, 1899/1900.
Medical Officer of Health reports 1856, 1858-1873, 1890-1900.
Rate assessments and valuation lists 1856-1900.
Vestry Clerk's Office:
>   Appointments of officers 1856-1900 (J).
>   Parliamentary schemes 1896-1900 (J).
>   Register of disorderly houses [Houses used for prostitution] 1888-1900 (J).
>   Vestry Clerk's copies of printed documents 1856-1876 (J).
Boundary marks register 1874.

BATTLE BRIDGE ESTATE PAVING, LIGHTING ETC. COMMISSIONERS
Minutes 1825-1855 (J).
[Part of the archives of the parish of St Pancras]

BEDFORD ESTATE PAVING, LIGHTING ETC. COMMISSIONERS
Minutes 1802-1855 (J).
Paving Act 1800 (J).
[Part of the archives of the parish of St Pancras]

BREWERS ESTATE PAVING, LIGHTING ETC. COMMISSIONERS
Minutes 1814-1855 (J).
[Part of the archives of the parish of St Pancras]

CALTHORPE ESTATE PAVING, LIGHTING ETC. COMMISSIONERS
Minutes 1814-1855 (J).
Rate assessments 1834-1854/55 (gaps) (J).
[Part of the archives of the parish of St Pancras]

CAMDEN TOWN ESTATE PAVING, LIGHTING ETC. COMMISSIONERS
Minutes 1822-1855 (J).
Qualification book 1824 (J).
Rate assessments 1822/23-1855/56 (gaps) (J).
[Part of the archives of the parish of St Pancras]

DOUGHTY ESTATE PAVING, LIGHTING ETC. COMMISSIONERS
Minutes 1827-1855 (J).
[Part of the archives of the parish of St Pancras]

FOUNDLING HOSPITAL ESTATE PAVING, LIGHTING ETC. COMMISSIONERS
Watch house report book 1827-1829.
Rate assessments 1855 (J).
[Part of the archives of the parish of St Pancras]

GLOUCESTER PLACE PAVING TRUST
Minutes 1827-1846 (J).
Ledger 1838-1841 (J).
Paving Act 1827 (J).
[Part of the archives of the parish of St Pancras]

HARRISON ESTATE PAVING, LIGHTING ETC. COMMISSIONERS
Minutes 1810-1855 (J).
Rate assessments 1821, 1822 (J).
[Part of the archives of the parish of St Pancras]

KENTISH TOWN PAVING, LIGHTING ETC. COMMISSIONERS
Minutes 1817-1855 (J).
Rate assessments 1852, 1855 (J).
[Part of the archives of the parish of St Pancras]

LUCAS ESTATE PAVING, LIGHTING ETC. COMMISSIONERS
Minutes 1810-1855 (J).
Rate assessments 1819, 1827, 1828, 1842-1855 (gaps) (J).
[Part of the archives of the parish of St Pancras]

ST PANCRAS PARISH UNION ESTATES PAVING, LIGHTING ETC. COMMISSIONERS
Minutes 1814-1855 (J).
[Part of the archives of the parish of St Pancras]

SKINNERS ESTATE PAVING, LIGHTING ETC. COMMISSIONERS
Minutes 1808-1855 (J).
Letterbook 1839-1855 (J).
Rate assessments 1851 (J).
[Part of the archives of the parish of St Pancras]

SOMERS TOWN ESTATE PAVING, LIGHTING ETC. COMMISSIONERS
Minutes 1789-1855 (J).
Rate assessments 1796, 1800, 1806, 1808 (J).
[Part of the archives of the parish of St Pancras]

SOUTHAMPTON ESTATE PAVING, LIGHTING ETC. COMMISSIONERS
Minutes 1812-1855 (J).
Surveyor's reports 1841-1849 (J).
Watch minutes 1818-1830 (J).
Rate assessments 1807-1855 (gaps) (J).
[Part of the archives of the parish of St Pancras]

SOUTH-WEST ST PANCRAS PAVING, LIGHTING ETC. COMMISSIONERS
Minutes 1773-1811, 1813-1816, 1832-1833, 1844-1855 (J).
Rate assessments 1773-1837 (gaps) (J).
[Part of the archives of the parish of St Pancras]

ST PANCRAS AND ISLINGTON BURIAL BOARD
Strawberry Vale Estate minutes 1877-1878 (J).

ST PANCRAS METROPOLITAN BOROUGH
Council minutes 1900-1965.
Committee minutes:
> Air Raid Precautions Emergency Committee 1936-1945 (J).
> Baths and Cemeteries Committee 1903-1907, 1916-1940 (J).
> Building Committee 1947-1965 (J).
> Contracts and Stores Committee 1926-1942 (J).
> Establishment and Public Buildings Committee 1945-1965 (J).
> Finance Committee 1904-1905, 1910-1912, 1917-1924, 1946-1965 (J).
> General Purposes Committee 1900-1928, 1932-1942, 1946-1965 (J).
> Highways, Sewers and Public Works Committee 1900-1965 (J).
> Housing Management [Estates] Committee 1922-1964 (J). *Closed until 50 years old.*
> Libraries and Arts [Education and Public Libraries] Committee 1904-1965 (J).
> Maternity and Child Welfare Committee 1945-1948 (J).
> Planning and Housing Development Committee 1949-1965 (J).
> Public Health Committee 1900-1965 (J).
> Road Safety Committee 1946-1964 (J).
> Staff Committee 1946-1965 (J). *Closed until 50 years old.*
> Valuation Committee 1940-1946 (J).
> Other committees 1900-1965 (J).

Annual reports and accounts 1901/02-1914/15.
Annual reports 1929/30-1938/39.
Annual accounts 1919/20-1944/45, 1949/50-1962/63.
General rates estimates 1955/56, 1957/58-1964/65.
Yearbooks [Almanac and diary] 1901, 1902, 1922, 1925-1945, 1946-1949, 1951-1955/56, 1957/58-1964/65.
Yearbooks and general information 1907, 1909-1915.
Borough Librarian's annual reports 1921/22, 1928/29-1937/38, 1955/56-1963/64.
Housing annual reviews 1957-1962, 1964.
Medical Officer of Health reports 1901-1938, 1945-1964.

Cemeteries records:

Joint account of St Pancras and Islington Cemeteries 1880-1967 (J).

Civil Defence records:

St Pancras air raid precautions personnel 1938-1945 (J).

Air raid precautions records including list of people killed 1940-1945 (J).

Department of Works:

Boundary mark queries 1947.

Mayor's Office:

Mayor's Local Charities (Cinema account) Fund Committee minutes 1916-1936 (J).

Town Clerk's Department:

Appointments of officers 1900-1946 (J).

St Pancras Local Tribunal [Deals with exemptions from military service] 1915-1916 (J).

Parliamentary schemes 1900-1913 (J).

Register of disorderly houses [Houses used for prostitution] 1900-1915 (J).

Rate assessments and valuation lists 1900-1965 (J).

11.4 London Borough of Camden

Council minutes 1964 to date.

Committee minutes 1964 to date (J).

Annual reports 1980/81-1985/86, 1994/95 to date.

Budget [General rates estimates] 1966/67-1988/89.

Capital programme 1985/86-1988/89.

Financial survey and accounts 1965/66-1972/73, 1974/75-1991/92, 1993/94 to date.

Diaries and yearbooks 1964/65 to date.

Libraries and Arts triennial reports 1965-1971.

Libraries and Information Service annual reports 1993/94, 1994/95.

Arts Services annual reports 1993/94, 1994/95.

Leisure and Community Services annual reports 1995/96 to date.

Medical Officer of Health reports 1965-1968.

Rate assessments 1965/66-1981/82 (J). *Closed until 30 years old.*

Valuation lists 1963 with amendments, 1973 with amendments up to 1989.

Mayor's Office:

Camden/Doncaster Twinning Association 1980s (J).

12. LOCAL RECORDS OF CENTRAL GOVERNMENT

LAND TAX COMMISSIONERS

Land Tax 1902/03. Metropolitan Borough of Holborn.

INLAND REVENUE

Duties on land values [Domesday Survey] 1909. Volumes covering the present London Borough of Camden (J).

13. RECORDS OF OTHER PUBLIC AUTHORITIES

HAMPSTEAD CITIZENS ADVICE BUREAU
Records 1950-1974 (J). *Closed until 50 years old.*

HAMPSTEAD COUNCIL OF SOCIAL SERVICES [formerly HAMPSTEAD COUNCIL FOR SOCIAL WELFARE]
Annual reports 1911-1962, 1965-1975.
Minutes 1952-1954.
Old Peoples Welfare Committee minutes 1946-1954.
Henderson House accounts and correspondence 1943-1954, 1960-1961.

HOLBORN UNION
Accounts 1886-1901, 1911-1914.
Annual report 1914.
[Archives of the Holborn Union held at London Metropolitan Archives, 40 Northampton Road, London EC1R 0HB]

KENTISH TOWN CITIZENS ADVICE BUREAU
Records 1950-1974 (J). *Closed until 50 years old.*

KING'S CROSS CITIZENS ADVICE BUREAU
Records 1950-1974 (J). *Closed until 50 years old.*

ST GILES IN THE FIELDS AND ST GEORGE'S BLOOMSBURY GUARDIANS OF THE POOR
Lists of the members 1901-1913.
Abstracts of accounts 1900/01-1912/13.
[Main archive at London Metropolitan Archives, 40 Northampton Road, London EC1R 0HB]

ST PANCRAS COUNCIL OF SOCIAL SERVICE [formerly PUBLIC WELFARE ASSOCIATION FOR SOUTHERN ST PANCRAS]
Minutes 1909-1934 (J).

ST PANCRAS GUARDIANS OF THE POOR
Official manual 1929/1930.
[Main archive held at London Metropolitan Archives, 40 Northampton Road, London EC1R 0HB]

SWISS COTTAGE CITIZENS ADVICE BUREAU
Records 1950-1974 (J). *Closed until 50 years old.*

WEST HAMPSTEAD CITIZENS ADVICE BUREAU
Records 1950-1974 (J). *Closed until 50 years old.*

16. RECORDS OF PARISHES

ST BARTHOLOMEW GRAYS INN ROAD
Papers regarding the amalgamation of parish with St George the Martyr Queen Square in 1959.

CHRIST CHURCH WOBURN SQUARE
Minutes 1830-1848.
Accounts 1830-1845.
[Part of the archives of the parish of St George Bloomsbury]

17. RECORDS OF NON-ANGLICAN PLACES OF WORSHIP

17.1 Non-conformist churches

LYNDHURST ROAD CONGREGATIONAL CHURCH, *Lyndhurst Road, Hampstead*
Register of marriages 1939-1976 (J).
Yearbooks 1883-1918, 1922-1931, 1934/35, 1936, 1961, 1966 (J).
Newsletters 1890-1947 (gaps) (J).
Other records include histories, lists of ministers etc. (J).

REGENT SQUARE CHURCH, *Regent Square, Bloomsbury, St Pancras*
Presbyterian church.
Young Men's Society minute book 1876-1881 (J).

TRINITY PRESBYTERIAN CHURCH, *High Street, Hampstead*
Register of marriages 1913-1919, 1947-1970 (J).

WHITEFIELD MEMORIAL CHURCH [Formerly WHITEFIELD'S TABERNACLE], *Tottenham Court Road, St Pancras*
Congregational church.
Register of marriages 1973-1977 (J).
Fellowship of Youth records 1929-1938 (J).

22. RECORDS OF ORPHANAGES, REFUGES AND PENITENTIARIES

HAMPSTEAD MOTHER AND BABY HOME, *17 Daleham Gardens, Hampstead*
Minutes and papers 1903-1970 (J)
Records of individual mothers, babies and adoptions 1953-1969. *Closed until 75 years old apart from records that do not name individuals.*

23. RECORDS OF SCHOOLS AND COLLEGES

HAMPSTEAD AND NORTH ST PANCRAS DAY NURSERY, *27-29 Pond Street, Hampstead*
Visitors book 1928.

KINGSGATE SCHOOL, *Kingsgate Road, Kilburn, Hampstead*
General evening institute correspondence book 1935-1939.
Honours book 1931/32-1939/40.
Roll of service 1914-1918.

MIDDLESEX STREET PRESBYTERIAN SCHOOL, *Middlesex Street, Somers Town, St Pancras*
Log book 1864-1874.

NETHERWOOD STREET SCHOOL, *Netherwood Street, Kilburn, Hampstead*
Evening classes log books 1885-1933.

NEW COLLEGE, *Finchley Road, Hampstead*
Congregational Theological College.
Annual reports and papers 1850s-1920s (J).

26. RECORDS OF CEMETERIES AND CREMATORIA

LONDON CEMETERY COMPANY [later UNITED CEMETERY COMPANY]
Highgate Cemetery registers 1839-1984.
Other Highgate Cemetery records 1839-1975.

29. RECORDS OF ASSOCIATIONS, CLUBS AND SOCIETIES

ARKWRIGHT ARTS TRUST, *Camden Arts Centre, Arkwright Road, Hampstead*
Minutes 1971-1975 (J).

ASSOCIATION FOR PROMOTING THE REPEAL OF TAXES ON KNOWLEDGE, *10 Ampton Place, St Pancras*
Opposed stamp duty on publications.
Papers 1830s-1850s (J).

BLOOMSBURY ASSOCIATION
Minutes, correspondence and publicity 1973-1993 (J).
Papers of George Wagner c.1973-1990s (J).

BLOOMSBURY COFFEE POT
One of a group of social clubs for people aged 21-35. Met at White Hart Public House, 128 Theobalds Road, Holborn.
Minutes, accounts and papers 1974-1980 (J).

BROAD STREET (RICHMOND LINE) COMMITTEE
The North London Line.
Papers 1970s-1980s (J).

CAMDEN CIVIC SOCIETY
Files and papers 1960s-1970s (J).

CAMDEN LABOUR PARTY
Files and papers 1969-1982 (J).

CAMDEN SQUARE GARDENS TRUSTEES, *Camden Town, St Pancras*
Minutes and other records 1865-1940 (J).

CHALCOT DISCUSSION SOCIETY, *Hampstead*
Women's discussion society.
Minutes, papers 1899-1950s (J).

ELEANOR PALMER CHARITY, *St Pancras*
Trustees' minutes 1927-1970 (J).
[Part of the archives of the London Borough of Camden]

FITZJOHNS AREA RESIDENTS' ASSOCIATION, *Hampstead*
Papers 1969-1974 (J).

GAYTON ROAD RESIDENTS' ASSOCIATION, *Hampstead*
Minutes, newsletters and papers 1971-1990 (J).

HAMPSTEAD ANTIQUARIAN AND HISTORICAL SOCIETY
Minutes, annual reports, cashbooks and papers 1897-1940.

HAMPSTEAD ASSEMBLY ROOMS, *Romney's House, Holly Bush Hill, Hampstead*
Minutes 1806-1844.
Papers and deeds 1800s.

HAMPSTEAD CHORAL SOCIETY
Programmes and papers 1949-1981 (J).

HAMPSTEAD CONSUMER GROUP
Papers 1960s (J).

HAMPSTEAD CONVERSAZIONE SOCIETY
Met at Hampstead Assembly Rooms, Romney's House, Holly Bush Hill, Hampstead.
Minutes 1846-1850.

HAMPSTEAD DINNER CLUB
Met at Hampstead Assembly Rooms, Romney's House, Holly Bush Hill, Hampstead.
Minutes 1784-1859.

HAMPSTEAD DISTRICT NURSING ASSOCIATION
Minutes 1929-1953.

HAMPSTEAD DIVISIONAL LIBERAL ASSOCIATION
Minutes 1938-1957.

HAMPSTEAD ETHICAL INSTITUTE, *Hampstead Conservatoire, 64 Eton Avenue, Hampstead*
Record of lectures 1900-1922.

HAMPSTEAD HIGH STREET AND ROSSLYN HILL IMPROVEMENT ASSOCIATION
Papers 1960s.

HAMPSTEAD LOCAL HISTORY SOCIETY
Local history and members indexes 1920s-1930s.

HAMPSTEAD MOTORWAY ACTION GROUP
Papers 1965-1978 (J).

HAMPSTEAD MUNICIPAL ELECTORS' ASSOCIATION
Minutes 1936-1945.

HAMPSTEAD MUNICIPAL OFFICERS' GUILD
Minutes 1910-1932 (J).
Committee attendance book 1919-1933 (J).
[Part of the archives of the Metropolitan Borough of Hampstead]

HAMPSTEAD NON-POLITICAL AND PROGRESSIVE ASSOCIATION
Cuttings books 1900-1919.

HAMPSTEAD PARLIAMENT
Debating society.
Debates, reports, correspondence and papers 1883-1939 (J).

HAMPSTEAD PUBLIC LIBRARY, *Stansfield House, Hampstead High Street, Hampstead*
Subscription Library.
Minutes and other records 1833-1966.

HAMPSTEAD ROTARY CLUB
Visitors book 1932-1948.

HAMPSTEAD WELLS AND CAMPDEN TRUST
Accounts 1859-1882 (J).
[Part of the archives of the parish of Hampstead]

HAMPSTEAD WELLS AND CAMPDEN TRUST
Letter books 1937-1966 (gaps) (J).
Other records 1783-1992 (J). *Not yet available.*
[Archives deposited by the Trust]

HEATH AND OLD HAMPSTEAD SOCIETY [formerly HAMPSTEAD HEATH PROTECTION SOCIETY]
Minutes and papers 1897-1980s (J).

HIGHGATE HARRIERS
Athletics club.
Minutes, photographs, medals and other records 1890s-1980s (J).

HOLBORN AND ST PANCRAS LABOUR PARTY
General Management Committee minutes 1948-1980 (J).
Executive Committee minutes 1948-1973 (J).
Other records 1961-1976 (J).

HOLBORN HOUSING ASSOCIATION
Association owned Bevan House, 36-39 Boswell Street, Holborn.
Minute book 1938-1960 (J).
Correspondence up to 1962 (J).

HOLBORN SOCIETY
Minutes and papers 1954-1966.

KENTISH TOWN MUTUAL IMPROVEMENT SOCIETY, *St Pancras*
Educational improvement society.
Papers c.1865-1897 (J).

KENTISH TOWN PARISH INSTITUTE, *St Pancras*
Minutes 1902-1909.

LINCOLN'S INN FIELDS TRUSTEES, *Holborn*
Ledgers, letterbooks and cashbooks 1735-1799.

LONDON MUNICIPALITIES FOOTBALL CLUB
Management committee minutes 1900-1913.
[Part of the archives of the Metropolitan Borough of Hampstead]

PLATT'S GIFT AND CHARLES' GIFT CHARITIES
Trustees' minutes and papers 1902-1970 (J).
[Part of the archives of the Metropolitan Borough of St Pancras]

RED LION SQUARE TRUSTEES, *Holborn*
Minutes and accounts 1846-1880.

ST PANCRAS BALL COMMITTEE
Minutes 1899-1912.

ST PANCRAS HOUSING ASSOCIATION
Photographs 1920s-1980s.
Other records 1920s-2000 (J).

ST PANCRAS SCHOOL FOR MOTHERS
Executive Committee minutes 1917-1925, 1936-1960.
[Part of the archives of the Metropolitan Borough of St Pancras]
Scrap book 1907-1916.

SOCIAL WELFARE ASSOCIATION FOR LONDON
Minute book 1911-1915.

SOCIETY FOR THE PRESERVATION OF OAKLEY SQUARE, *Camden Town, St Pancras*
Papers 1960s.

STOCKS CHARITY, *Hampstead*
Minutes 1780-1947 (J).
[Part of the archives of the Metropolitan Borough of Hampstead]

TORRINGTON SQUARE TRUSTEES, *Bloomsbury, Holborn*
Papers 1820s-1918.

UNITED LAW DEBATING SOCIETY
Minutes, correspondence, and papers 1881-1964 (J).
Also includes records of its predecessors, the Law Students' Debating Society founded 1836 and
United Law Society founded 1864.

30. RECORDS OF THEATRES AND CINEMAS

HAMPSTEAD CHILDREN'S CINEMA COUNCIL
Minutes and papers 1954-1957 (J).

HAMPSTEAD THEATRE
Programmes and other records 1960s-1980s (J). *Some records unavailable.*

UNITY THEATRE, *Goldington Street, Somers Town, St Pancras*
Playbills, programmes, cuttings, newsletters and scripts c.1944-1947 (J).

UNITY THEATRE SCHOOL, *Goldington Street, Somers Town, St Pancras*
Minutes 1946–1947 (J).

33. RECORDS OF BUSINESSES

DAVIS AND SONS, *209 Tottenham Court Road, Bloomsbury, Holborn*
Furniture manufacturers from c.1875.
Accounts and order books 1900s-1930s (J).

EVANS, Lewis, *2 Osnaburgh Street, Regent's Park, St Pancras*
Chemist.
Prescription books 1895-1912, 1922-1943 (J).

HAMPSTEAD SAVINGS BANK, *High Street, Hampstead*
Rules and regulations 1863.

HILGER, Adam, *Kings Road Works, Camden Town, St Pancras*
Manufacturers of laboratory and technical equipment.
Accounts, order books and other records 1900s-1920s (J).

LEVERTON AND SONS, *212 Eversholt Street, Camden Town, St Pancras*
Funeral directors.
Records of associated companies:
      Renfree [formerly Nodes]. 1871-1905 (J).
      Tarbucks [formerly Dickens].1855-1864, 1868-1912 (J).
      Other records 1896-1905, 1955 (J).

POTTERS, *47 Heath Street, Hampstead*
Estate agent.
Cash books 1917-1932, 1974-1975 (J).
Rentals 1967-1973 (J).
Insurance records 1957-1970 (J).

SEXTON, SONS AND ASHBY, *Bank Chambers, 42 Kilburn High Road, Kilburn, Hampstead*
Architects.
Day books and various plans 1900-1967 (J).

STAMP, E.B., *29 Hampstead High Street, Hampstead*
Chemist.
Prescription book 1929-1930.

WILSON, Edwin, *51-102 Chenies Mews, Bloomsbury, Holborn*
Removals contractor and repository.
Letterbooks, accounts and other records c.1898-1912 (J).

34. FAMILY AND PERSONAL PAPERS AND RECORDS OF PRIVATE ESTATES

BARRATT, Thomas J., *Bellmoor, East Heath Road, Hampstead*
Local historian and antiquarian.
Papers relating to him and his house 1890s-1910s (J).

FORTUNE GREEN AND WEST END GREEN, *West Hampstead, Hampstead*
Papers concerning court cases over the ownership of the greens 1870s-1890s (J).

HAWLEY ESTATE, *Camden Town, St Pancras*
Papers and deeds c.1830s-1840 (J). *Mainly concerns acquisition for railway use by East and West India Docks Railway [later called North London Railway].*

HOARE, John Gurney
Transcripts of court cases and other papers concerning dispute with Sir Thomas Maryon Wilson about the ownership of Hampstead Heath and other documents 1560-1869, compiled 1866-1869.
[See p.68 for extracts from the Hampstead Manor Court rolls]

PRATT, Charles, *Earl Camden*
Terrier book for his Camden Town estate, St Pancras 1807-c.1919.

STEVENSON, John
Heathkeeper on Hampstead Heath.
Diary 1834-1840.

SWINTON ESTATE, *King's Cross, St Pancras*
Papers and deeds c.1815-c.1847.

VINCENT, Robert
Book of plans of the property of Robert Vincent in Hampstead by Isaac Messeder 1773.

35. MANORIAL RECORDS

HAMPSTEAD
Copy of minute books 1742-1843.
[Archives of Hampstead Manor held at London Metropolitan Archives, 40 Northampton Road, London EC1R 0HB]
[See also p.44]

ST ANDREW HOLBORN ABOVE BARS AND ST GEORGE THE MARTYR QUEEN SQUARE

Court Leet minutes 1817-1841 and Court Leet accounts 1813-1836.

[Part of the archives of the Vestry of St Andrew Holborn above Bars and St George the Martyr Queen Square]

36. MANUSCRIPTS AND MANUSCRIPT COLLECTIONS

36.1 Literary manuscripts

CONNELL, John
Chairman of St Pancras Education and Public Libraries Committee.
Manuscript of biography of W.E. Henley, winner of 1949 James Tait Black memorial prize.

DENYER, C.H.
Typescript of 'St Pancras through the centuries' edited by C.H. Denyer, with papers and photographs of St Pancras pageant 1931.

GEE, Christina and HOLDER, Marjorie
Typescript and papers for the 'Diary of a London Schoolboy 1826-1830' written by John Thomas Pocock, published 1980.

PARTON, John
'Some account of the hospital and parish of St Giles in the Fields' 1815. Original manuscript. His book of the same title was published in 1822.

THOMPSON, F.M.L.
Typescript of 'Hampstead: the building of a borough', published 1974.

WISWOULD, Samuel
'Some account of Kentish Town' 1821. Manuscript copy.

36.2 Collections of autographed material

BAILLIE, Joanna, *near Red Lion Hill, Hampstead (c.1799-c.1820); Bolton House, Windmill Hill, Hampstead (c.1820-1851)*
Author.
Collection of letters written by her 1810s-1840s.

BARCLAY, Edgar, *Wycombe Studios, King Henry's Road, Hampstead; Elm Row, Hampstead (1869-1912)*
Local artist. Member of Hampstead Heath Protection Society.
Collection of letters written by him from Algiers, Tlemcen and Kabylia 1872-1880.
Portfolio of drawings.

MAXWELL, Anna E.
Novelist and local historian.
Collection of papers about her 1833-1899.

MONTAGU, *Lady* **Mary Wortley**
Wife of 3rd Earl of Bute, owner of Kenwood House until 1755.
Collection of letters written by her on her travels abroad in Europe, Asia and Africa 1710s-1720s.

36.3 Other documents and manuscripts

KENWOOD HOUSE, *Hampstead Lane, St Pancras*
Catalogue of the library at Kenwood House 1802, checked by the Library 1829.

SEVEN DIALS, *Holborn*
Plan of the proposed development of Seven Dials, St Giles in the Fields, 1693.

STUKELEY, William
Plan and details of the estate of Revd Dr William Stukeley, including land and property in Kentish Town, St Pancras 1764.

37. ANTIQUARIANS' COLLECTIONS

37.1 Monumental inscriptions

ANON
Transcriptions of monumental inscriptions for St John Hampstead 1870.

CAMDEN HISTORY SOCIETY
Transcriptions and plans of monumental inscriptions for St John Hampstead, 1976-1986. *Buried in Hampstead* (1986) describes the Camden History Society inscriptions and those by James Milward and L.B. Snell.

CANSICK, Frederick Teague
Transcriptions of monumental inscriptions for Foundling Hospital [orphanage] Chapel 1871, Highgate Chapel Burial Ground 1886, St Andrew Holborn Burial Ground, Gray's Inn Road 1884-1885, St George Bloomsbury Burial Ground 1885, St George the Martyr Queen Square Burial Ground 1885, St Giles in the Fields 1877, St James Hampstead Road c.1880s, St Martin's Burial Ground, Camden Town [St Martin in the Fields] 1888, St Pancras Old Church and Churchyard 1877, 1880 and other churches in St Pancras 1889, 1892.

MILWARD, James
Transcriptions of monumental inscriptions for St John Hampstead, collected for Robert Hovenden by James Milward 1881.

SNELL, L.B.
Transcriptions of monumental inscriptions for St John Hampstead, [n.d.]. Covers letters A, B and P only.

37.2 Other collections

BELLMOOR COLLECTION
A companion to Thomas Barratt's 'Annals of Hampstead', published 1912. 21 vols.

HAMPSTEAD MANOR
Extracts from the Hampstead Manor Court Rolls 1607-1843.
[See p.65 for transcripts and papers relating to Hoare v. Wilson case]

HEAL COLLECTION
Large collection created by Sir Ambrose Heal (of Heal's furniture firm) about the parish of St Pancras, including maps, books, documents, illustrations, newscuttings and playbills (particularly for Scala Theatre). Donated in 1913. Separate index.

38. COPIES OF SOURCE MATERIAL HELD ELSEWHERE

ST JOHN HAMPSTEAD [Church Row]
Registers:
      Baptism 1560-1840.
      Marriage 1560-1837.
      Burial 1560-1842.
Trustees' minutes 1797-1934.
[Microfilm of originals held by incumbent]

London Borough of Ealing

Ealing Local History Centre
Ealing Central Library
103 Ealing Broadway Centre
London
W5 5JY

Tel:
020-8825 8194

Fax:
020-8840 2351

E-mail:
libuser@ealing.gov.uk

Website:
www.ealing.gov.uk/libraries

Location:
Central Library is above Safeway in Ealing Broadway Centre.
Lifts for the disabled.

Nearest station:
Ealing Broadway (Thames Trains, Central and District Lines)

Parking:
Car parking is available in the shopping centre.

Days of opening:
Tuesday - Saturday.

Administrative history:
The London Borough of Ealing comprises the former boroughs of Acton, Ealing and Southall. Before 1965 the whole area was in the county of Middlesex.

The ancient parishes in the area were: Acton, Ealing (Old Brentford part of parish in London Borough of Hounslow), Greenford, Hanwell (New Brentford part in London Borough of Hounslow), Hayes (Norwood part of parish, later Southall), Northolt, Perivale and West Twyford (extra parochial district of parish of Willesden). The rest of Hayes parish is the London Borough of Hillingdon. Local Boards were created in a number of areas from the 1860s. These were abolished in 1894 when urban and rural district councils were established.

The Uxbridge Poor Law Union covered the parishes of Hanwell, Northolt and Norwood (Southall). The Brentford Poor Law Union covered the parishes of Acton, Ealing, Greenford and Perivale.

Catalogues and indexes

Indexes to books, pamphlets, archives, journals and other miscellany.

Index to monumental inscriptions for St Mary Acton, St Mary Ealing, St Mary Norwood and St Mary Perivale.

Research guides:

OATES, J.D., *Guide to sources for family history* (1999).

Postal and telephone enquiries:

Lengthy research not undertaken; enquirers will be encouraged to visit or to employ a records agent.

Services:

Photographic service; reproduction fees charged, usually waived for non-commercial organisations.

Photocopying facilities including black and white laser copies; archives and fragile items may not be copied.

Microfilm/fiche reader/printer.

Talks and lectures to school classes and local groups.

Related collections held elsewhere:

GUNNERSBURY PARK MUSEUM
Gunnersbury Park
Pope's Lane
London
W3 8LQ
Artefacts of many aspects of local life and work, oral history collection, photographs, illustrations and ephemera.
Open afternoons.

THE HERITAGE CENTRE
Ravenor Farm
29 Oldfield Lane South
Greenford
Middlesex
UB6 9LB
Reference library of items about the history of Middlesex, and collection of 20th century artefacts.
Open weekends.

PITSHANGER MANOR AND GALLERY
Mattock Lane
Walpole Park
Ealing
London
W5
Collections of Martinware sculptures.

ST BERNARD'S HOSPITAL MUSEUM
Ealing Hospital
Uxbridge Road
Southall
Middlesex
Artefacts relating to the former County Asylum.
Open by appointment.

SOUTHALL LIBRARY
Osterley Park Road
Southall
Middlesex
UB2 4BL
Collections of the Martinware sculptures.

1. BOOKS, PAMPHLETS AND PERIODICALS

Books relating to the borough's history, including histories of local organisations, biographies and reminiscences of local people, basic histories of neighbouring areas and works on the history of London and Middlesex. Works of fiction or other works by local authors are not collected, unless they have a local setting.

Local periodicals of all kinds including parish magazines.

Victoria County History:
Middlesex vol. 3 - Greenford and Hanwell.
Middlesex vol. 4 - Northolt, Norwood (Southall) and Perivale.
Middlesex vol. 7 - Acton, Ealing and West Twyford.

3. NEWSPAPERS

BUCKINGHAMSHIRE ADVERTISER 1854-1874.

EALING ILLUSTRATED MAGAZINE 1858-1859; continued as EALING PARISH MAGAZINE 1860-1861; continued as EALING POST 1866-1868.

MIDDLESEX COUNTY TIMES 1868-1974; continued as EALING GAZETTE 1974-1989; continued as EALING AND ACTON GAZETTE 1989 to date.
Indexed 1866-1961, 1972-1986.

ACTON GAZETTE 1871-1988.
Continued as the Ealing and Acton Gazette (see above)
Indexed 1870-1965, 1972-1986.

SOUTHALL NEWS 1885-1888.

EALING GAZETTE 1888-1923.

SOUTHALL AND NORWOOD GAZETTE 1894-1923; continued as WEST MIDDLESEX GAZETTE 1923-1941; continued as MIDDLESEX COUNTY TIMES AND WEST MIDDLESEX GAZETTE 1941-1954; continued as MIDDLESEX COUNTY TIMES [SOUTHALL EDITION] 1954-1974; continued as SOUTHALL GAZETTE 1974 to date.
Indexed 1972-1986.

EALING GUARDIAN 1898-1900.

HANWELL GAZETTE 1898-1923.

ACTON EXPRESS 1900-1911; continued as THE ACTON AND CHISWICK GAZETTE 1912-1918.

EALING NEWS 1936.

GREENFORD AND NORTHOLT GAZETTE 1974 to date.
Indexed 1972-1986.

MIDWEEK COUNTY TIMES 1969-1974; continued as MIDWEEK GAZETTE 1974-1981.

4. CUTTINGS COLLECTIONS

Collection of nineteen scrapbooks containing miscellaneous information about local history. Most indexed.

5. DIRECTORIES

5.2 London, county and general directories

MIDDLESEX
Pigot and Co.
1822-1840 (gaps).

MIDDLESEX
Kelly's
1845-1937 (gaps).

5.3 Local directories

ACTON
Kellys.
1927-1940.

ACTON
Kent Service Ltd.
1955.

BRENTFORD
Jacksons.
1877.
Includes Ealing.

CHISWICK
Kellys.
1915-1926, 1940.
Includes Acton until 1927.

EALING
Mason's.
1853.

EALING AND HANWELL
Cordingly's.
1881.

EALING
Kellys.
1887-1940 (gaps).

EALING AND HANWELL
Kemps.
1949-1975.

EALING
Thomsons.
1981 to date.

HARROW
Kelly's.
1915-1924. Extracts for Greenford, Northolt, Perivale, West Twyford.

SOUTHALL
King's.
1896.

SOUTHALL
King's Gazette Almanack.
1900.

5.4 Telephone directories

5.4.2. Local areas

EALING
1971 to date.

EALING, HOUNSLOW AND DISTRICT
1955-1970 (gaps).

5.4.3 Yellow pages

LONDON NORTH WEST
1973 to date.

6. ELECTORAL REGISTERS

ACTON
1918, 1921-1964.

EALING [including ACTON, GREENFORD and PERIVALE]
1890-1914.

EALING
1919-1965 (gaps).

HARROW
1931, 1938 (Greenford, Hanwell and Northolt only), 1939 (Greenford only).

UXBRIDGE
1928 (Northolt only).

LONDON BOROUGH OF EALING [including ACTON and SOUTHALL]
1965 to date.

7. ILLUSTRATIONS

Paintings and prints about 1200 to date. Most are of views of the borough and its residents from the late nineteenth and early twentieth centuries. Indexed.

Almost 20,000 photographs of people, places and scenes of life within the borough. More photographs of Ealing and Acton than in the more northern and rural (until the 1930s) parts of the borough. Topographical catalogue. Images of people, events and objects catalogued separately.

Collection of slides. Indexed.

8. MAPS

8.1 General maps

Local maps, including John Rocque's map of 1741-1745. Copies of maps of Middlesex 1575-1891.

Copies of tithe maps for Ealing 1839, Northolt 1838, Perivale 1839. Copies of parish maps for Acton 1805, Ealing 1778, 1822, Greenford 1814, Hanwell 1803, Northolt 1835, Norwood 1821.

Plans of Northolt Racecourse, 1935-1936. Goad shopping plans 1967 to date.

8.2 Ordnance Survey maps

5 INCHES: 1 MILE (1: 12,500)
c.1950.

6 INCHES: 1 MILE (1: 10,560); 1:10,000 (approx. 6 inches: 1 mile)
c.1867, c.1894, c.1912, 1930s, c.1966, c.1975.

25 INCHES: 1 MILE
c.1865, c.1894, c.1914, c.1935.

60 INCH: 1 MILE (1: 1,056)
c.1894. Parts of Acton and Ealing.

1: 1,250 (approx. 50 inches: 1 mile)
1950s-1970s.

11. LOCAL AUTHORITY RECORDS AND RECORDS OF PREDECESSOR AUTHORITIES

11.1 Acton Borough area

ACTON PARISH
Vestry minutes and accounts 1801-1868.
Highway Surveyors' accounts 1775-1811.
Charity records 1612-1900.
Rate assessments 1751, 1755, 1796-1797, 1826, 1836.
Graves register 1864-1950.

ACTON LOCAL BOARD
Board minutes 1865-1894.
Committee minutes:
       Drainage Committee 1883-1888.
       Finance Committee 1866-1905.
       Highways Committee 1868.
       Works and Roads Committee 1872-1905.
       Other Committees 1885-1905.

ACTON URBAN DISTRICT COUNCIL
Council minutes 1895-1921.
Committee minutes:
       Cemetery Committee 1896-1905.
       Coronation Celebrations Committee 1911-1912.
       Education Committee 1909-1921.
       Electricity Committee 1904-1905.
       Fire Brigade Committee 1899-1901.
       Health and Isolation Hospital Committee 1904-1905.
       Highways, Lighting and Control Committee 1904-1905.
       Horse and Cartage Committee 1897-1901.
       Law and Parliamentary Committee 1896-1901.
       Sanitary Committee 1901-1904.
       Works Committee 1901-1905.

ACTON BOROUGH
Council minutes 1921-1965.
Committee minutes:
Committees 1936-1965.
Council and Staff Joint Committee 1940-1964.
Education Committee 1921-1965.
Road Safety Committee 1961-1964.
Housing Department articles, agreements, contracts and plans 1930-1957.

11.2 Ealing Borough area

EALING PARISH
Vestry minutes and notices 1797-1927.
Highway Committee minutes 1769-1874.
Poor Law records:
> Overseers' minutes 1898-1926.
> Poor rate and disbursement books 1674-1744.

Rate assessments 1744-1836.
Charity records 1819-1925.
Census returns: heads of households 1801, 1811. *Indexed.*

HANWELL PARISH
Vestry minutes 1780-1926.
Churchwardens' accounts 1766-1835.
Vestry and Burial Board letter book 1882-1902.
Burial Board minutes and accounts 1881-1903.
Poor Law records:
> Overseers' accounts 1790-1801.
> Poor relief books 1814-1853.

Highway Surveyors' book 1775-1815.

EALING LOCAL BOARD
Board minutes 1863-1894.
Committee minutes:
> Baths Committee 1886-1905.
> Electric Lighting Committee 1892-1900.
> Finance Committee 1869-1894.
> Public Library Committee 1883-1899.
> Sanitary Committee 1878-1894.
> Works Committee 1869-1897.
> Other Committees 1887-1892.

HANWELL LOCAL BOARD
Board minutes 1885-1896.
Committee minutes:
> Finance Committee 1885-1894.
> Highways Committee [including Letter Books] 1881-1885.

EALING URBAN DISTRICT COUNCIL
Council minutes 1895-1902.
Committee minutes:
> Electric Lighting Committee 1900-1903.
> Finance Committee 1895-1901.
> Fire Brigade Committee 1893-1906.

General Purposes Committee 1897-1901.
Housing Committee 1899-1914.
Public Library Committee 1899-1907.
Queen Victoria's Diamond Jubilee Commemoration Fund Committee and Victoria Hall Organ
Fund Sub-Committee 1898-1903.
Sanitary Committee 1900-1904.
Works Committee 1897-1904.

GREENFORD URBAN DISTRICT COUNCIL
Greenford U.D.C. became part of the Borough of Ealing in 1926.
Council minutes 1895-1926.
Plans and Buildings Committee minutes 1923-1926.

HANWELL URBAN DISTRICT COUNCIL
Hanwell U.D.C. became part of the Borough of Ealing in 1926.
Council minutes 1896-1926.
Committee minutes:
    Allotments Committee 1920-1926.
    Finance Committee 1895-1913.
    Finance Establishment Committee 1914-1926.
    Fire Brigade Committee 1913-1925.
    General Purposes Committee 1903-1926.
    Maternity and Child Welfare Committee 1918-1926.
    Public Health Committee 1917-1926.
    Public Library Committee 1904-1926.
    Public Lighting Committee 1904-1926.
    Sanitary Committee 1899-1913.

EALING BOROUGH
Council minutes 1901-1965.
Committee minutes:
    Air Raid Precautions Committee 1938-1939.
    Allotment Garden Committee 1922-1965.
    Baths Committee 1902-1928.
    Baths and Fire Brigade Committee 1928-1947.
    Baths, Victoria Hall and Public Buildings Committee 1931-1965.
    Civic Restaurants Committee 1942-1947.
    Civil Defence Committee 1939-1965.
    Economy of Manpower Committee 1947.
    Education Committee 1903-1965.
    Electricity Supply Committee 1902-1948.
    Entertainments Committee 1946-1965.
    Finance Committee 1901-1965.
    Fire Brigade Committee 1902-1928.
    General Purposes Committee 1901-1940.

General Purposes and Establishment Committee 1940-1965.
Gunnersbury Park Joint Committee 1928-1965.
Highways and Open Spaces Committee 1901-1904.
Highways, Open Spaces and Tramways Committee 1902-1956.
Housing Committee 1903-1965.
Local Government Reorganisation Committee 1963-1964.
Maternity and Child Welfare Committee 1926-1934.
National Emergency Committee 1914-1919.
National Registration Committee 1915-1916.
Parliamentary Committee 1903-1907.
Profiteering Committee 1919-1921.
Public Health Committee 1902-1965.
Public Library Committee 1907-1965.
Public Relations Committee 1948-1955.
Rating and Valuation Committee 1927-1951.
Recreation and Sports Committee 1920-1965.
Recruiting Committee 1915-1921.
Savings Committee 1929-1932.
Town Planning and Buildings Committee 1928-1965.
Victoria Hall Management Committee 1899-1939.
War Memorials Committee 1947-1952.
War Memorials Trustees Fund 1919-1930.
Welfare Committee 1921.
Works Committee 1904-1956.
Works and Highways Committee 1956-1965.
Other Committees 1906-1965

11.3 Southall Borough area

NORWOOD PARISH
Part of parish of Hayes until 1859.
Churchwardens' accounts 1676-1879.
Burial Board minutes 1881-1899.
Highway Board minutes 1873-1891.
Nuisances Removal Committee 1856-1859.
Sanitary Committee minutes 1877.
Poor Law records:
>   Overseers' accounts 1826-1840, 1867-1908 (gaps).
>   Poor Rate and disbursement books 1653-1826.
Rate assessments 1774-1881, 1884.
Charity records 1720-1962.
Lighting inspectors' accounts 1881-1891.

SOUTHALL-NORWOOD LOCAL BOARD

Board minutes 1891-1894.
Committee minutes:
>	Byelaws, Legal and Parliamentary Committee 1891-1894.
>	Finance Committee 1891-1892.
>	Works and Sanitary Committee 1891-1894.

SOUTHALL-NORWOOD URBAN DISTRICT COUNCIL

Council minutes 1895-1936.
Committee minutes:
>	Allotment Committee 1910-1935.
>	Burial Board Committee 1897-1931.
>	Bye Laws Committee 1895-1935.
>	Cemetery, Parks and Open Spaces Committee 1932-1934.
>	Finance Committee 1895-1935.
>	General Purposes Committee 1920-1935.
>	Hospital Committee 1911-1923.
>	Housing Committee 1924-1935.
>	Housing and Town Planning Committee 1910-1932.
>	Library Committee 1905-1933.
>	Parks and Pleasure Grounds Committee 1904-1909.
>	Public Health Committee 1921-1935.
>	Staff Committee 1928-1935.
>	Works and Sanitary Committee 1895-1921.

SOUTHALL BOROUGH

Council minutes 1936-1965.
Committee minutes:
>	Air Raid Precautions and Civil Defence 1938-1965.
>	Comforts and Welfare in Wartime Committee 1941-1947.
>	Entertainments Committee 1947-1965.
>	Establishment Committee 1935-1965.
>	Finance Committee 1935-1965.
>	General Purposes Committee 1935-1965.
>	Housing Committee 1935-1965.
>	Parks and Open Spaces Committee 1935-1965.
>	Public Health Committee 1935-1965.
>	Public Library Committee 1935-1965.
>	Rating and Valuation Committee 1935-1950.
>	Works and Highways Committee 1935-1965.
>	Other Committees 1940-1965.

11.4 London Borough of Ealing

Council minutes 1965 to date.

16. RECORDS OF PARISHES

HOLY CROSS GREENFORD
Vestry minutes 1912-1921.

17. RECORDS OF NON-ANGLICAN PLACES OF WORSHIP

17. 1 Non-conformist churches

ACTON UNITED REFORMED CHURCH, *Churchfield Road, Acton, Middlesex*
Deeds 1868-1977.

FEDERAL COUNCIL OF EALING FREE CHURCHES
Minutes, cash books, attendance registers and scrapbooks 1923-1999.

HANWELL WESLEYAN METHODIST CHAPEL, *Boston Road, Hanwell; Church Road, Hanwell, Middlesex*
Leaders' meetings minutes, Trustees' minutes and accounts 1882-1969.

21. RECORDS OF HOSPITALS, ASYLUMS AND DISPENSARIES

ACTON COTTAGE HOSPITAL, *Gunnersbury Lane, Acton, Middlesex*
Minute books, annual reports, accounts 1898-1975.

22. RECORDS OF ORPHANAGES, REFUGES AND PENITENTIARIES

HOME FOR MOTHERLESS CHILDREN, *Warwick Road, Ealing, Middlesex*
Deeds 1891-1939.
Correspondence and notes 1936-1965.

23. RECORDS OF SCHOOLS AND COLLEGES

ACTON CENTRAL SENIOR SCHOOL, *Shakespeare Road, Acton, Middlesex*
Log book 1905-1957.

ACTON COUNTY SCHOOL, *Woodlands, Acton, Middlesex*
Governors' minutes 1903-1919.

ACTON GREEN FIRST AND MIDDLE SCHOOL, *Acton, Middlesex*
Log and accident books 1978-1992.

ACTON JUNIOR MIXED SCHOOL (ST MARY'S), *Oldham Terrace, Acton, Middlesex*
Log book 1926-1932.

ACTON PRIORY BOY'S SCHOOL, *Acton Lane, Acton, Middlesex*
Log books 1883-1950.

ACTON PRIORY GIRLS' SCHOOL, *Acton Lane, Acton, Middlesex*
Log books 1899-1937.

ACTON PRIORY INFANTS' SCHOOL, *Acton Lane, Acton, Middlesex*
Log books 1920-1981.

ACTON PRIORY SECONDARY MODERN SCHOOL, *Acton Lane, Acton, Middlesex*
Log book 1950-1961.

ACTON PRIORY SENIOR GIRLS' SCHOOL, *Acton Lane, Acton, Middlesex*
Log book 1937-1959.

ACTON ST MARY'S BOYS' SCHOOL, *Oldham Terrace, Acton, Middlesex*
Log books 1862-1926.

ACTON ST MARY'S GIRLS' SCHOOL, *Oldham Terrace, Acton, Middlesex*
Log books 1862-1922.

ACTON ST MARY'S INFANTS' SCHOOL, *Oldham Terrace, Acton, Middlesex*
Log books 1862-1920.

ACTON SPECIAL SCHOOL, *School Road, Acton, Middlesex*
Log book and admission register 1915-1972.

ACTON WELLS JUNIOR MIXED AND INFANT SCHOOL, *School Road, Acton, Middlesex*
Log books 1900-1980.

ALLENBY ROAD INFANTS' SCHOOL, *Allenby Road, Southall, Middlesex*
Log book 1932-1934.

ARUNDELL JUNIOR SCHOOL, *Hartfield Avenue, Northolt, Middlesex*
Log book 1953-1980.

ARUNDELL PRIMARY INFANTS' SCHOOL, *Hartfield Avenue, Northolt, Middlesex*
Log book 1953-1960.

BEAUMONT PARK JUNIOR GIRLS' SCHOOL, *Acton Lane, Acton, Middlesex*
Teachers' account books, log books 1933-1981.

BERRYMEDE INFANTS' SCHOOL, *Osborne Road, Acton, Middlesex*
Log book 1931-1950.
Stock books 1926-1945.

BISCOE SCHOOL, *Tentelow Lane, Southall, Middlesex*
Daily attendance and register books, class registers 1860-1950.

BYRON HOUSE SCHOOL, *The Park, Ealing, Middlesex*
Correspondence and accounts 1862-1876.

CASTLEBAR SCHOOL, *Hathaway Gardens, Ealing, Middlesex*
Log book 1980-1987.

COSTON JUNIOR BOYS' SCHOOL, *Oldfield Lane, Greenford, Middlesex*
Log books 1931-1974.

COSTON JUNIOR GIRLS' SCHOOL, *Oldfield Lane, Greenford, Middlesex*
Log book 1938-1974.

COSTON SCHOOL, *Oldfield Lane, Greenford, Middlesex*
Log book 1928-1968.

COSTON SECONDARY GIRLS' SCHOOL, *Oldfield Lane, Greenford, Middlesex*
Log book 1969-1974.

DORMERS' WELLS JUNIOR, MIXED AND INFANT SCHOOL, *Dormers Wells, Southall, Middlesex*
Log book 1934-1938.

EALING BOYS' NATIONAL SCHOOL, *Ealing Green, Ealing, Middlesex*
Log book 1872-1891.

EALING COUNTY SCHOOL FOR BOYS, *Ealing Green, Ealing, Middlesex*
Admission and staff registers 1913-1981.

EALING DRAYTON BOYS' SCHOOL, *Drayton Grove, Ealing, Middlesex*
Visitors' book 1908-1931.

EALING DRILL HALL INFANTS' SCHOOL, *Somerset Road, Ealing, Middlesex*
Log book 1904-1905.

EALING GRANGE SCHOOL, *Church Place, Ealing, Middlesex*
Log book 1925-1947.

EALING GRANGE SECONDARY MODERN SCHOOL, *Church Place, Ealing, Middlesex*
Log book 1947-1966.

EALING LAMMAS INFANTS' SCHOOL, *Cranmer Avenue, Ealing, Middlesex*
Log book 1910-1954.

EALING LAMMAS PRIMARY SCHOOL, *Cranmer Avenue, Ealing, Middlesex*
Log book 1954-1958.

EALING LAMMAS SCHOOL, *Cranmer Avenue, Ealing, Middlesex*
Log book 1904-1905.

EALING MEAD SCHOOL, *Almond Avenue, Ealing, Middlesex*
Log books 1965-1974.

EALING ST MARY'S BOYS' SCHOOL, *South Ealing Road, Ealing, Middlesex*
Log books 1891-1934.

EALING ST MARY'S GIRLS' SCHOOL, *Ealing Green, Ealing, Middlesex*
Log books 1871-1926.

EALING ST MARY'S INFANTS' SCHOOL, *South Ealing Road, Ealing, Middlesex*
Log book 1888-1922.

EALING ST MARY'S JUNIOR MIXED SCHOOL, *South Ealing Road, Ealing, Middlesex*
Log book 1935-1941.

EALING ST STEPHEN'S SCHOOL, *Pitshanger Lane, Ealing, Middlesex*
Log books 1897-1931.

EAST ACTON JUNIOR SCHOOL, *East Acton Lane, Acton, Middlesex*
Log book 1926-1931.

THE ELMS SECONDARY SCHOOL, *Twyford Crescent, Acton, Middlesex*
Log book 1957-1961.

FEATHERSTONE COUNTY SCHOOL, *Featherstone Road, Southall, Middlesex*
Log books 1958-1971.

FEATHERSTONE ROAD MANUAL TRAINING CENTRE, *Featherstone Road, Southall, Middlesex*
Log book 1911-1946.

FEATHERSTONE ROAD SCHOOL, *Featherstone Road, Southall, Middlesex*
Log books 1895-1942.

GREENFORD TEMPORARY JUNIOR MIXED AND INFANTS' SCHOOL, *near Allenby Road, Greenford, Middlesex*
Log book 1939-1942.

HANWELL BRITISH SCHOOL, *Westminster Road, Hanwell, Middlesex*
Log books 1871-1902.

HANWELL WESTMINSTER ROAD JUNIOR SCHOOL, *Westminster Road, Hanwell, Middlesex*
Log book 1904-1906.

HORSENDEN SECONDARY BOYS' SCHOOL, *Horsenden Lane, Greenford, Middlesex*
Log book 1969-1975.

HORSENDEN SENIOR BOYS' SCHOOL, *Horsenden Road, Greenford, Middlesex*
Log book,1935-1968.

JOHN PERRYN INFANTS' SCHOOL, *Long Drive, East Acton, Acton, Middlesex*
Log book 1931-1940.

JOSEPH LANCASTER INFANTS' SCHOOL, *Lancaster Road, Ealing, Middlesex*
Log book 1901-1906.

JOSEPH LANCASTER SCHOOL, *Lancaster Road, Ealing, Middlesex*
Log books 1919-1925.

LADY MARGARET ROAD INFANTS' SCHOOL, *Lady Margaret Road, Southall, Middlesex*
Log book 1938-1968.

LITTLE EALING BOYS' SCHOOL, *Little Ealing Lane, Ealing, Middlesex*
Log book 1905-1929.

NORTH EALING BOYS' SCHOOL, *Pitshanger Lane, Ealing, Middlesex*
Log book 1931-1934.

NORTHFIELDS BOYS' SCHOOL, *Balfour Road, Ealing, Middlesex*
Log book 1905-1953.

NORTHFIELDS FIRST SCHOOL, *Balfour Road, Ealing, Middlesex*
Log books 1976-1981.

NORTHFIELDS INFANTS' SCHOOL, *Balfour Road, Ealing, Middlesex*
Log book 1905-1956.

NORTHFIELDS MIDDLE SCHOOL, *Balfour Road, Ealing, Middlesex*
Log book 1975-1981.

NORTHFIELDS SECONDARY GIRLS' SCHOOL, *Balfour Road, Ealing, Middlesex*
Log book 1905-1948.

NORTHOLT CHURCH OF ENGLAND SCHOOL, *Northolt, Middlesex*
Log books 1866-1914.

OAKLANDS ROAD INFANTS' SCHOOL, *Oaklands Road, Hanwell, Middlesex*
Log books 1906-1942.

PERIVALE SECONDARY GIRLS' SCHOOL, *Sarsfield Road, Perivale, Middlesex*
Log book 1971-1975.

PERIVALE SELBORNE FIRST SCHOOL, *Conway Crescent, Perivale, Middlesex*
Log books 1974-1980.

PERIVALE SELBORNE PRIMARY SCHOOL, *Conway Crescent, Perivale, Middlesex*
Log books 1935-1974.

PERIVALE SENIOR BOYS' SCHOOL, *Sarsfield Road, Perivale, Middlesex*
Log book 1936-1968.

PERIVALE (SENIOR) GIRLS' SCHOOL, *Sarsfield Road, Perivale, Middlesex*
Log book 1937-1971.

ROTHSCHILD ROAD INFANTS' SCHOOL, *Acton Green, Acton, Middlesex*
Log books, admission registers and punishment books 1904-1981.

ST ANN'S COOKERY CENTRE, *Springfield Road, Hanwell, Middlesex*
Log book 1926-1934.

ST ANN'S SECONDARY BOYS' SCHOOL, *Springfield Road, Hanwell, Middlesex*
Log books 1902-1937.

ST ANN'S SECONDARY GIRLS' SCHOOL, *Springfield Road, Hanwell, Middlesex*
Log books 1903-1981.

SOUTH ACTON INFANTS' SCHOOL, *Osborne Road, Acton, Middlesex*
Log books 1890-1931.

SOUTHALL CLIFTON ROAD BOYS' SCHOOL, *Clifton Road, Southall, Middlesex*
Log books 1908-1935.

SOUTHALL COUNTY SCHOOL, *Villiers Road, Southall, Middlesex*
Governors' minutes 1907-1931.

SOUTHALL WESTERN ROAD INFANTS' SCHOOL, *Western Road, Southall, Middlesex*
Log books 1911-1958.

SOUTHFIELD INFANTS' SCHOOL, *Bedford Park, Acton, Middlesex*
Log books, school journals, summaries 1906-1993.

TALBOT SPECIAL SCHOOL, *Talbot Road, Southall, Middlesex*
Log book 1936-1966.

THOMAS HUXLEY COLLEGE, *Woodlands Avenue, Acton, Middlesex*
Minutes, prospectuses, curriculum,1966-1980.

TUDOR PRIMARY GIRLS' SCHOOL, *Tudor Road, Southall, Middlesex*
Log books 1938-1956.

TUDOR ROAD SENIOR MIXED SCHOOL, *Tudor Road, Southall, Middlesex*
Log book 1907-1938.

27. RECORDS OF FIRE AND SALVAGE BODIES

ACTON VOLUNTEER FIRE BRIGADE, *Acton High Street, Acton, Middlesex*
Records 1868-1921.

EALING FIRE BRIGADE, *Uxbridge Road, Ealing, Middlesex*
Records 1895-1934.

28. RECORDS OF MILITARY AND ARMED BODIES

EALING AND BRENTFORD VOLUNTEERS
Records 1798-1965.

29. RECORDS OF ASSOCIATIONS, CLUBS AND SOCIETIES

1895 ASSOCIATION
Records 1946-1986.

ACTON 10-15 CLUB
Minutes 1937-1938.

ACTON ART SOCIETY
Records 1951-1965.

ACTON CHRYSANTHEMUM, DAHLIA AND FLORAL ART SOCIETY
Records 1950-2001.

ACTON LIBERAL CLUB, *8 Avenue Road, South Acton, Acton, Middlesex*
Minutes 1887-1890.

ACTON LITERARY INSTITUTE, *Acton High Street, Acton, Middlesex*
Records 1868-1889.

ACTON LOCAL HISTORY SOCIETY
Records 1961-1965, 1986-1990.

ACTON PHOTOGRAPHIC SOCIETY
Records 1904-1924.

ACTON SCHOOLS' MUSIC ASSOCIATION
Minutes 1946-1966.

ALL HALLOWS' YOUTH CLUB, *Horsenden Lane, Greenford, Middlesex*
Records 1959-1964.

ASSOCIATION FOR THE OCCUPATION OF THE ELDERLY
Minutes 1969-1974.

BADEN POWELL LODGE, *Acton, Middlesex*
Minutes 1900-1911.

EALING AND ACTON OPERATIC SOCIETY
Records 1935-1936.

EALING CHESS CLUB
Records 1885-1974.

EALING CONSERVATIVE CLUB
Register 1888-1907.

EALING MICROSCOPICAL AND NATURAL HISTORY SOCIETY
Records 1877-1934.

EALING MUSEUM, ART AND HISTORY SOCIETY
Records c.1900-2002.

EALING PAROCHIAL CHARITIES
Records 1690-1932.

EALING RESIDENTS' ASSOCIATION
Records 1965-1974.

EALING SWIMMING CLUB
Records 1882-1934.

EALING TENANTS' LTD
Records 1901-1974.

EALING TOXOPHOLITES
Constitution 1795.

EALING WAR DRESSINGS FUND
Records 1915-1919.

GREATER EALING LOCAL HISTORY SOCIETY
Records 1956-1973.

GREENFORD LIBRARY DISCUSSION GROUP
Records 1942-1955.

HANWELL ORDER OF THE SONS OF TEMPERANCE
Records 1886-1927.

HANWELL PRESERVATION SOCIETY
Records 1848-1999.

LAMMAS PARK BOWLING CLUB, *Lammas Park, Ealing, Middlesex*
Membership List 1907.

LEAGUE OF NATIONS UNION: EALING BRANCH
Records 1919-1945

MAGPIE LAWN TENNIS CLUB, *Castlebar Hill, Ealing, Middlesex*
Records 1883-1888.

MISS JAY'S LEGACY TO THE POOR
Correspondence 1947-1948.

NORTH HANWELL RESIDENTS' ASSOCIATION
Records 1933-1974.

30. RECORDS OF THEATRES AND CINEMAS

BANKSIDE LITTLE THEATRE, *Tring Avenue, Ealing, Middlesex*
Records 1928-1976.

33. RECORDS OF BUSINESSES

GREENSLADE PAPERS
Correspondence and other records relating to the Martin Brothers' pottery works at Southall c.1873-1933.

HAVEN GREEN CAB RANK, *Haven Green, Ealing, Middlesex*
Correspondence 1877-1967.

SOUTHALL BRICKFIELD SITE, *Greenford Avenue, Southall, Middlesex*
Letters, plans and reports 1922.

STROUD'S BRICKFIELD, *Acton, Middlesex*
Partnership documents 1894, 1898.

34. FAMILY AND PERSONAL PAPERS AND RECORDS OF PRIVATE ESTATES

BROWN, John Allen (1831-1903)
Antiquarian, local author and amateur historian. Founder of Ealing Free Library.
Correspondence, journals and newscuttings 1822-1901.

GRUNDY, John Hull (1907-1984)
Professor of Natural History, artist and collector of Martinware.
Diaries, correspondence, notes 1923-1970.

ST JOHN, Henry Algernon Francis (1911-1979)
Civil servant, former Acton County schoolboy.
Diaries 1922-1968.

WETHERALL, *General Sir* **Frederick Augustus (1754-1842)**
Soldier. Served in America, Canada, India, Gibraltar and West Indies. ADC to Duke of Kent, godfather of Queen Victoria.
Correspondence 1800-1898.

37. ANTIQUARIANS' COLLECTIONS

37.2 Other collections

KEEN, Charles Keene
Transcripts and notes relating to Northolt 1728-1984.

PUGH PAPERS
Notes 1898-c.1960.

JONES, M.E.R.
Scrapbook of letters and articles, many by or about M.E.R. Jones, an Ealing resident (1878-c.1960).
Indexed.

Ealing Broadway

Regent's Canal, Hoxton, 1950

London Borough of Hackney

Hackney Archives Department
43 De Beauvoir Road
London
N1 5SQ

Tel:
020-7241 2477

Fax:
020-7241 6688

E-mail:
archives@hackney.gov.uk

Website:
www.hackney.gov.uk

Location:
At intersection of De Beauvoir Road and Downham Road.
Disabled access.

Nearest stations:
Liverpool Street (Anglia Railways, First Great Eastern, WAGN Railways, Circle, Hammersmith and City and Central Lines) 2 miles; Dalston Kingsland (Silverlink Railways) 1200metres.

Parking:
Unrestricted parking in surrounding streets.

Days of opening:
Tuesday, Wednesday, Thursday and Friday by appointment only.

Administrative history:
The London Borough of Hackney comprises the former Metropolitan Boroughs of Hackney, Shoreditch and Stoke Newington. The whole area was in the County of Middlesex before 1889 and in the County of London 1889-1965.

The ancient parishes in the area were: Hackney, Shoreditch and Stoke Newington, part of the parish of South Hornsey and part of the extra-parochial liberty of Norton Folgate.

Between 1855 and 1894 most functions within the parishes of Hackney and Stoke Newington were administered by the Hackney District Board of Works. On the dissolution of the Board of Works in 1894, its functions reverted to the respective vestries. Shoreditch was administered by its elected vestry from 1855-1900. South Hornsey was administered by the South Hornsey Board of Works 1855-1894. This was replaced by South Hornsey Urban District Council 1894-1900.

The Hackney Poor Law Union covered the parishes of Hackney and Stoke Newington 1834-1930 and also South Hornsey 1900-1930. In Shoreditch the Poor Law was administered by the Shoreditch Trustees for Maintaining the Poor until 1868 and by Shoreditch Union until 1930. South Hornsey formed part of the Edmonton Union until 1900, and Norton Folgate was part of Whitechapel Union for the same period.

Holdings:
Records of London Borough of Hackney and its predecessor authorities. Material inherited from the Hackney, Shoreditch and Stoke Newington Local Studies collections. Deposited records that have an association with the Hackney area. Local history library, visual collection and oral history tapes.

Catalogues and indexes:
Official and deposited records: Lists; subject and topographical indexes; field name index; personal names index. Ratebook street index (selected books only).
Map index.
Local history collections: Author/class catalogues. Index to Shoreditch and Stoke Newington cuttings books. Directories catalogue.
Visual collections: Card catalogue arranged topographically and by subject.
Oral history collection: Card catalogue of cassette copies by name of subject. Card catalogue of complete collection by tape number.
Computerised cataloguing system for local history material available during 2005.

Research guides:
TAYLOR, M., *Registers and burial grounds*, (1998).
Free leaflets on various subjects including registers and burial grounds, sources for genealogists, voters lists, maps, ratebooks and newspapers.

Services:
Scanning service; reproduction fees charged; no personal photography allowed.
Copies of digitised images (black and white and colour).
Photocopying facilities (black and white); some items may not be copied.
Microfilm/fiche reader/printers.
Publications on sale, including books, maps, posters and postcards; list available; postal service.
Research service; fees charged.

1. BOOKS, PAMPHLETS AND PERIODICALS

Books relating to Hackney, Stoke Newington and Shoreditch, with some general London material. Works of local history and topography; material by authors with local associations; works of fiction relating to the Hackney area. Writings of Edgar Allan Poe, Daniel Defoe and Isaac Watts.

Pamphlets on similar themes. Printed ephemera, in particular programmes and bills from local theatres.

Periodicals relating to archives and family history. Local periodicals including magazines and journals of parish and other religious institutions, schools and local organisations, such as trade unions.

Victoria County History:
Middlesex vol. 10 – Hackney and Stoke Newington

Selected books on other areas:
MANDER, D., *Hackney: strength in the tower* (1995).
MANDER, D., *More light, more power* (1996).
MANDER, D., *Stoke: look backwards, look forwards* (1997).

2. SPECIAL COLLECTIONS OF PRINTED MATERIAL

JOHN DAWSON LIBRARY
Collection built up by an excise man who lived in Hoxton. Donated to St Leonard's Church, Shoreditch, in 1765.
Scientific, theological, topographical and general works.

THEATRE BILLS AND POSTERS
Bills, posters and cuttings concerning theatres including Alexandra Theatre, Stoke Newington, Britannia Theatre, Hoxton, City of London Theatre, Dalston Theatre, Grecian Theatre, Shoreditch, Hackney Empire, National Standard Theatre [later Olympia Theatre], Shoreditch, Varieties Theatre, Shoreditch 1826-1956.

3. NEWSPAPERS

Most local newspapers are available on microfilm from which copies may be made.

THE CRAFTSMAN 1749-1752.

HOXTON SAUSAGE AND JERRY WAGS JOURNAL 1826.

HACKNEY AND CLAPTON MAGAZINE 1829.

HACKNEY MAGAZINE AND PARISH REFORMER 1833-1838.

TOWER HAMLETS MAGAZINE OR THE PUBLIC AND DOMESTIC MISCELLANY OF POLITICS, LITERATURE AND COMMERCE 1834.

HACKNEY MAGAZINE 1837-1838, 1858.

HACKNEY JOURNAL 1842.

HOXTON MAGAZINE OR RELIGIOUS AND MORAL INSTRUCTOR 1843.

BRITISH WORKMAN 1855-1868.

HACKNEY EXPRESS AND SHOREDITCH OBSERVER 1857-1879; continued as HACKNEY EXPRESS 1883-1903; continued as SHOREDITCH OBSERVER 1904-1915.

EASTERN POST 1868-1938.

HACKNEY AND KINGSLAND GAZETTE 1869-1909; continued as HACKNEY GAZETTE 1909 to date.
Indexed 1869-1881, 1965-1982.

LITTLE VENTILATOR 1869-1873; continued as THE VENTILATOR 1873-1904.

WORKMAN'S CLUB JOURNAL 1875-1878.

HACKNEY MERCURY 1885-1891, 1893-1910.

NORTH LONDON GUARDIAN 1888-1916.

EAST LONDON MAGAZINE 1890-1893.

HACKNEY AND STOKE NEWINGTON RECORDER 1909-1925.

HACKNEY SPECTATOR 1910-1911.

SUFFRAGETTE 1912-1915; continued as BRITANNIA 1915-1918.

WORKER'S DREADNOUGHT 1914-1924

HACKNEY MONTHLY AND STOKE NEWINGTON AND STAMFORD HILL REVIEW 1919-1920.

NORTH LONDON RECORDER 1927-1929, 1936-1937.

NORTH LONDON OBSERVER 1939-1940; continued as STOKE NEWINGTON AND HACKNEY OBSERVER 1940-1971.

STOKE NEWINGTON PEOPLE'S PAPER 1970-1971.

HACKNEY GUTTER PRESS 1971-1974.

SOUTH HACKNEY POST 1971-1972, 1979.

HACKNEY ACTION 1972-1973; continued as HACKNEY PEOPLE'S PRESS 1973-1984.

HACKNEY HERALD 1974-1988; continued as HACKNEY TODAY 1988 to date.
Newspaper of Hackney Council.

PIG'S EAR: THE EAST LONDON BEER DRINKERS' PAPER 1980-1981.

4. CUTTINGS COLLECTIONS

Collections for Hackney 1898-1964 (and some 18th century and earlier 19th century material), Stoke Newington 1858, 1889-1895, 1900-1956, Shoreditch 1893, 1895-1965 and Hoxton and Haggerston 1710-1852. Most Hackney cuttings before 1945 are mostly about official matters.

5. DIRECTORIES

5.1 Court guides

ABC COURT DIRECTORY
1871.

5.2 London, county and general directories

ESSEX, HERTFORDSHIRE, KENT, MIDDLESEX, SURREY AND SUSSEX
Kelly's.
1852, 1855, 1859, 1878.

LONDON
The Little London Directory.
1677.

LONDON
Complete guide.
1760, 1777.

LONDON
Post Office (Various publishers until 1836; from 1837 Kelly's).
1804, 1808, 1817, 1819, 1821, 1822, 1824, 1829, 1832 (extract), 1833, 1835, 1838, 1842, 1844-1847, 1850, 1855, 1861, 1873-1875, 1877, 1880, 1883, 1886, 1890, 1892, 1895, 1899, 1901, 1904, 1911, 1917, 1920, 1930, 1934, 1937, 1939-1943, 1945-1972, 1975-1980, 1982-1986.

LONDON
Kent's.
1814, 1823.

LONDON
Johnstone's.
Hackney section.
1817

LONDON
Pigot's.
1822, 1823, 1825, 1826, 1835, 1839.

LONDON
Robson's.
1828, 1831, 1839.

LONDON
Post Office Suburban (Kelly's).
1860, 1865-1866, 1911.

MIDDLESEX
Kelly's.
1867, 1871, 1882, 1886, 1890, 1912.

5.3 Local directories

DALSTON
Kelly's.
1894-1895, 1898, 1900-1901, 1905-1908.
Includes Kingsland, De Beauvoir Town and Cannonbury.

HACKNEY
Hackney Almanack and Directory.
1843.

HACKNEY AND STOKE NEWINGTON
Caleb Turner until 1851; from 1853 various publishers.
1845, 1847, 1849, 1851, 1853, 1855, 1867.

HACKNEY AND NORTH EAST LONDON
Green.
1869.

HACKNEY
Brabner.
1872.

HACKNEY
Kelly's.
1887-1889, 1890, 1894-1896, 1898, 1900, 1902, 1905, 1907-1915.

HIGHBURY
Kelly's.
1884-1888, 1893-1897, 1915.
Includes Stoke Newington, Stamford Hill and Clapton until 1889.

LOWER AND UPPER CLAPTON
Ellis.
1882.

STAMFORD HILL AND TOTTENHAM
Kelly's.
1899, 1901, 1908.

STOKE NEWINGTON AND CLAPTON
Green's.
1866.

STOKE NEWINGTON
Ellis.
1876, 1878, 1880, 1884.

STOKE NEWINGTON
Norris.
1882, 1883, 1884.

STOKE NEWINGTON
Kelly's.
1890-1891, 1894, 1898-1906, 1908-1916, 1918-1919, 1921-1929.
Includes Stamford Hill, Upper and Lower Clapton.

TOTTENHAM
Kelly's.
1923.

6. ELECTORAL REGISTERS

HACKNEY
1834, 1841, 1871, 1889 (Central Hackney only), 1901-1902, 1918-1964.

SHOREDITCH
1843, 1845, 1879, 1897-1964.

SOUTH HORNSEY
1879.

STOKE NEWINGTON [including SOUTH HORNSEY 1883-1964]
1861, 1879, 1883, 1893-1964.

LONDON BOROUGH OF HACKNEY
1964 to date.

7. ILLUSTRATIONS.

Views of the London Borough of Hackney. About 21,000 items excluding deposited and official holdings of visual material.

The Hackney on Disk database provides access to digitised copies via keyword searches and by using digitised Ordnance Survey maps. At present some 12,000 images are available.

8. MAPS

8.1 General maps

General maps of London, maps of parishes and the metropolitan boroughs, surveys of estates, sale plans and tithe maps. The earliest detailed maps of the Hackney area (apart from a small map of southern Shoreditch of 1559) date from 1745. These are Peter Chassereau's Map of Shoreditch and John Rocque's Survey of Hackney and Stoke Newington. Tithe maps of Hackney 1843 and Stoke Newington 1848.

8.2 Ordnance Survey maps

6 INCHES: 1 MILE (1: 10,560)
1848. Hackney and Stoke Newington. Skeleton survey.
1935. Hackney, Shoreditch and Stoke Newington. Geological survey.

25 INCHES: 1 MILE
1868-1872, 1894-1896, 1914-1916, 1936.

60 INCHES: 1MILE (1: 1,056)
1868-1872, 1894-1896, 1914-1916, 1907-1921, 1934-1938. (incomplete).

1: 1,250 (approx. 50 inches: 1 mile)
1948 to date (incomplete).
Borough atlas 1966, 1972, 1998. Includes most recent sheets for whole borough.

9. AUDIO-VISUAL ITEMS

About 50 films and videos, the earliest of which is a short film of the Hoxton and Shoreditch area 1920.

40 oral history tapes, recorded in 1980s, about living and working in Hackney prior to 1945. Some transcripts available.

10. COLLECTIONS OF MUSEUM OBJECTS

CRAMP FAMILY
Microscope and slides of biological samples c.1900.

11. LOCAL AUTHORITY RECORDS AND RECORDS OF PREDECESSOR AUTHORITIES

11.1 Hackney Metropolitan Borough area

HACKNEY PARISH
Vestry minutes 1771-1883.
Parish Meeting/Inhabitants' minutes 1762-1835.
Parish Treasurer's accounts with parish officers 1737-1798.
Parish Banker's accounts with the parish trustees 1765-1769.
Churchwardens and Overseers' accounts 1732-1823 (gaps).
Highway, paving and watching records:
      Highways Board minutes 1836-1856.
      Surveyors' record books (labour used) 1734-1804 (gaps).
      Other records 1720-1783, 1843.
St John at Hackney Lamp and Watch Trustees records:
      Minutes 1828-1837.
      Financial records 1764-1835 (gaps).
      Other Records 1825-1828.
Poor Law records:
      Trustees of the Poor minutes 1764-1900.
      Survey, Finance and Finance and Default Committees minutes 1850-1900 (gaps).
      Workhouse Committee minutes 1741-1787 (gaps).
      Treasurer and Overseers' financial records 1716-1815 (gaps).
      Apprenticeship registers 1767-1797.
      Workhouse financial records and out relief payments 1739-1804 (gaps).
      Examinations and settlements c.1720-1760.
      Applications for poor relief registers 1821-1822.
      Parish poor children registers 1762-1800 (gaps).

Workhouse inmates registers 1753-1767.
Other records 1741, 1755-1764, 1770-1807.
Rate assessments 1716-1743 (gaps), 1736-1842, 1856-1859.
Land Tax assessments 1727, 1730-1779, 1781-1784, 1787-1810, 1812-1822, 1824.
Census returns: heads of households 1811, 1821 and 1831.
Army of Reserve rate book and record of payments to substitutes 1803, 1805.
Other records 1712-1761, 1803-1819, 1839-1871.

HACKNEY VESTRY
Vestry minutes 1855-1900.
Committee minutes:
Baths and Washhouses Committee 1891-1900.
Electric Lighting Committee 1896-1900.
Lammas Lands and Charity Lands Committee 1855-1856.
Law and Parliamentary Committee 1887-1902.
Survey (Valuation) Committee 1894-1899.
Town Hall Committee [later Charities and Parochial Property Committee] 1893-1901.
Annual reports 1895-1900.
Clerk's records:
Correspondence 1855-1898.
Electoral records 1871-1894.
Medical Officer of Health correspondence 1895-1897.
Surveyor's records:
Letterbooks 1894-1900.
Street lists (including specifications for cleaning) 1895-1900.
Valuations lists 1875-1900.

HACKNEY BOARD OF WORKS
Board minutes 1855-1894.
Committee minutes:
Finance Committee 1863-1894.
General Purposes Committee 1856-1890.
Open Spaces Committee 1880-1896.
Sanitary Committee 1875-1878.
Street Regulation Committee 1891-1899.
Town Hall [later House Committee] 1862-1873, 1885-1896.
View Committee 1872-1877.
Annual reports 1856-1894.
Byelaws, special reports 1857-1893.
Surveyor's Department records 1855-1894.

HACKNEY METROPOLITAN BOROUGH
Minutes 1900-1965.
Committee minutes:
Air Raid Precautions Committee [later Civil Defence Committee] 1938-1939, 1950-1965.

Allotments Committee 1955-1961.
Baths Committee 1921-1949.
Baths and Civic Recreation Committee 1949-1965.
Civic Entertainments Committee 1945-1959.
Civil Defence and Finance Committee 1940-1950.
Economy Committee 1931-1932.
Electricity Committee 1909-1948.
Electric Lighting Committee 1900-1909.
Emergency Committee 1939-1940.
Establishment and General Purposes Committee 1900-1964.
Finance Committee 1900 -1940, 1950-1965.
Housing Committee [later Housing and Town Planning Committee] 1919-1965.
Joint (Staffs) Committee 1936-1964.
Legal and Parliamentary Committee 1902-1914, 1928-1958.
Local Joint (Works) Committee for Employees 1936-1953.
Local Savings Committee 1951-1964.
Maternity and Child Welfare Committee 1919-1948.
Open Spaces Committee 1900-1906, 1912-1914.
Post War Reconstruction Committee 1942-1953.
Public Health Committee 1900-1965.
Public Libraries Committee 1904-1965.
Safety First Committee 1937-1965.
Survey and Valuation Committee [later Rating Committee] 1901-1949.
Tenders Committee 1912-1914.
Town Hall and Library Committee 1901, 1903-1914.
Works and General Purposes Committee 1900-1914.
Works and Open Spaces Committee 1914-1965.
Annual reports 1901-1914, 1923, 1934-1939.
Abstracts of accounts 1939-1965.
Diaries and yearbooks 1904-1960 (gaps).
Librarian's reports 1904-1965.
Medical Officer of Health annual reports 1900-1963.
Mayoral files 1919-1964.
Baths and Civic Recreation Department records:
Accounts 1918-1927.
Other records 1900-1964.
Civil Defence records 1939-1963.
Electricity Undertaking records:
Accounts 1925-1948.
Other records 1912-1939.
Engineer and Surveyor's Department records:
Compulsory Purchase Orders 1930-1950.
Contract records and accounts 1927-1967.
Deposited plans 1864-1924.
Drainage and sewer records 1855-1940.

Maps and plans 1920-1937.
Out letter books and operational files 1900-1965.
Public Health Department:
    Inspection and licensing records 1922-1960.
    Maternity and child welfare records 1930-1965.
    Slum clearance records 1928-1955.
    Staffing records 1909-1955.
Public Libraries records:
    Administration records 1907-1964.
    Cuttings books 1826-1966.
Rate assessments and valuation lists 1903-1965.
Land tax assessments 1939-1949.

11.2 Shoreditch Metropolitan Borough area

SHOREDITCH PARISH
Vestry minutes 1727-1853
Committee minutes:
    Baths and Washhouses Committee 1852-1855.
    Burial Board 1855-1872, 1891-1896.
    Commissioners of Pavements 1840-1846.
Burial Board reports 1855-1858.
Finance Committee report 1825.
Churchwardens, Overseers and Ratepayers' Meetings minutes 1859-1885.
Churchwardens' accounts 1829-1855.
Poor Law records:
    Abstracts of accounts 1818-1819, 1831-1836, 1858, 1860-1872.
    Account of rents 1817-1828.
    Casual relief list 1843.
    Workhouse meat supplies 1825-1826.
Four Rates Board records:
Collected rates for lighting, roads, paving and policing in Shoreditch.
    Minutes 1778-1851.
    Ledgers 1823-1859.
    Ratebooks 1807-1810, 1819-1848.
    Report books 1828-1830.
Watchmen's books 1825-1830.
Charity Trustees' records 1764–1900.
Charity Schools' minutes 1705-1888
Census returns: abstract of data 1831.
Letterbook 1852-1855.
Land tax assessment ledgers 1744-1812, 1815-1826.

SHOREDITCH VESTRY

Vestry minutes 1855-1900.

Committee minutes:

Assessment Committee 1863-1900.

Baths and Washhouses Committee [later Baths and Washhouses Commissioners] 1855-1857, 1887-1899.

Dusting and Scavenging Committee [Lighting and Scavenging Committee] 1891-1900.

Electrical Lighting Committee 1893-1900.

Finance Committee 1856-1900.

General Purposes and Sanitary Committee 1857-1900.

Housing of the Working Classes Committee 1891-1900.

Lighting, Cleansing and Paving Committee 1856-1861.

Parliamentary (and Improvement) Committee 1867-1886, 1891-1900.

Paving Committee 1885-1893.

Paving and Sewers Committee 1893-1897.

Public Library Commissioners [later Public Library Committee] 1891-1900.

Sewers Committee 1856-1861.

Technical Instruction Committee 1892-1896.

Town Hall Committee 1863-1900.

Valuation Committee 1870-1900.

Works Committee 1897-1900.

Annual reports and accounts 1856-1900.

Housing of the Working Classes Committee reports and accounts 1892-1896.

Medical Officer of Health reports 1857, 1887-1888, 1893-1900.

Parliamentary (and Improvement) Committee accounts 1891-1900.

Town Hall Committee reports 1865-1868, 1891-1895.

Finance Department correspondence 1899-1900.

Surveyor's records:

Fire engineer's report book 1866.

Pavement contracts 1892-1894.

Paving correspondence 1891-1893.

Sewer accounts 1859-1866, 1891-1896.

Surveyor's report book 1856.

Vestry Clerk's records:

Correspondence 1856-1901.

Administration of electoral registers and voting records 1857-1901.

Rate assessments and valuation lists 1844-1900.

SHOREDITCH METROPOLITAN BOROUGH

Council minutes 1900-1965

Committee Minutes:

Assessment Committee 1901-1949.

Baths Committee 1900-1953, 1962-1965.

Charity Committee 1901-1909.

Cleansing and Transport Committee 1900-1902, 1948-1965.

Electricity Committee 1900-1948.
Establishment Committee [later General Purposes Committee] 1900-1965.
Finance Committee 1901-1963 (gaps).
Highway and Works Committee 1900-1958 .
Housing Committee 1900-1964.
Law and Parliamentary Committee 1929-1939.
Maternity and Child Welfare Committee 1920-1948.
Public Health Committee 1900-1965 (gaps).
Public Libraries Committee 1900-1965.
Reconstruction Committee 1941-1948.
Staffing Committee 1920-1927, 1935-1964.
Valuation Committee 1900-1950.
Welfare Committee 1947-1965.

Annual reports 1900-1937.
Abstracts of accounts 1900-1962.
Electrical Engineer's reports 1946-1947.
Librarian's annual reports 1900-1964.
Medical Office of Health reports 1901-1963.
Mayor's correspondence 1914, 1920-1933.
Baths Department records 1899-1952.
Civil Defence records 1936-1953.
Engineer and Surveyor's Department records 1901-1960 (gaps).
Public Libraries Department records:
Administration records 1900-1965.
Cuttings collection 1892-1965.
Town Clerk's letter books 1902-1947.
Rate assessments and valuation lists 1902-1965.
Rate summons 1907-1948.
Register of local land charges 1925.
Property assessment registers 1900-1930.

11.3 Stoke Newington Metropolitan Borough area

STOKE NEWINGTON PARISH
Vestry minutes 1681-1743, 1784-1895.
Lists of vestrymen and rate returns 1883-1895.
Committee Minutes:
Burial Board 1862-1896.
Board of Health 1831-1832.
Churchwardens' accounts 1840-1916.
Highway and paving records:
Accounts and report 1831-1837.
Vouchers 1830-1853.
Poor Law records:
Accounts 1862-1897.

Examinations 1786-1805.
List of paupers employed 1831.
Other records 1824, 1836-1839.
Rate assessments 1822-1848.
Charity records 1764–1904.
National Parochial School records 1898–1911.

STOKE NEWINGTON VESTRY
Vestry minutes 1895-1900.
Committee Minutes:
Finance Committee 1894-1898.
General Purposes Committee 1894-1900.
Library Commissioners 1890-1898.
Sanitary Committee 1896-1899.
Annual reports 1894-1900.
Income and expenditure accounts 1898-1899.
Rate assessments and valuation lists 1862, 1858-1901.

SOUTH HORNSEY LOCAL BOARD OF HEALTH [SOUTH HORNSEY URBAN DISTRICT COUNCIL (1894-1900)]
Minutes 1865-1900.
Committee Minutes:
Board [Council] Committee 1887-1900.
Finsbury Park Free Public Library Committee 1891-1898.
General Purposes Committee 1867-1900.
Inspectors for Lighting Albert Town 1854-1865.
Joint Representation Committee 1900-1901.
Library Committee 1898-1900.
Medical Officer of Health reports 1898-1900.
Surveyor's report 1890-1900.
Regulations and list of officers' duties 1876.
Surveyor's records 1866-1900.
Treasurer's records 1867-1900.

STOKE NEWINGTON METROPOLITAN BOROUGH
Council agendas and minutes 1900-1965.
Committee minutes:
Air Raid Precautions [Civil Defence Committee] 1938-1965.
Assessment Committee 1930-1935.
Council and Staff Advisory Joint Committee 1923-1963.
Electricity Committee 1904-1940, 1944-1948.
Emergency Committee 1939-1944.
Establishment Committee 1937-1965.
Finance Committee 1899-1965.
General Purposes Committee 1901-1965.

Highways and Sewers Committee 1900-1940, 1944-1965.
Housing Committee 1933-1965.
London Government Re-organisation Committee 1958-1964.
Maternity and Child Welfare Committee 1922-1940, 1944-1948.
Public Baths Committee 1933-1940, 1944-1965.
Public Health Committee 1899-1940, 1944-1965.
Public Library Committee 1900-1933, 1945-1965.
Rating and Valuation Committee 1908-1947.
Town Planning Committee 1946-1952.
Works and Building Committee 1953-1965.
Annual reports 1900-1938.
Financial statements and abstracts of accounts 1900-1929, 1933-1965.
Council diaries and yearbooks 1919-1965.
Bath Superintendent's reports 1957-1961.
Borough Librarian's reports 1900-1964 (gaps).
Electricity undertaking accounts 1919-1948.
Medical Officer of Health reports 1900-1963.
Officers' reports 1934-1953.
Mayor's records 1914-1922, 1949-1965.
Civil Defence Department records 1939-1965.
Engineer and Surveyor's Department records:
Air raid precaution administration files 1937-1945.
Street improvements records 1902-1957.
Street trading records 1939-1960.
Public Health Department records 1900-1955.
Public Libraries Department records 1889-1900, 1904-1965.
Town Clerk's records 1900-1964.
Treasurer's Department:
War loan and damage records 1917-1918, 1940-1948.
Rate assessments and valuation lists 1898-1964 (gaps).

11.4 London Borough of Hackney

Council minutes 1964 to date.
Committee minutes 1964-1989. *Closed until 30 years old. Housing Committee closed until 25 years old. Confidential presented papers not available.*
Annual revenue estimates and abstracts of accounts 1971 to date.
Baths and Civic Recreation Department reports 1966-1974.
Borough Librarian's report 1968-1974.
Medical Officer of Health reports 1964-1973.
Borough Solicitor's Legal Services records:
Title deeds of properties purchased by the London Borough of Hackney and its constituents c.1680-c.1950.
Architects Department records:
Plans of council properties 1934-1978. *Closed until 30 years old.*

Plans of the De Beauvoir Town council estate 1968-1973.

Provisional fair rent assessment (by house and street) 1973 to date.

Directorate of Technical and Contract Services records:

Applications for new streets and street projections 1856-1971.

Building and drainage plans 1856-1985. *Closed until 30 years old.*

Correspondence files 1954-1985. *Closed until 30 years old.*

Rate assessments 1966-1968.

12. LOCAL RECORDS OF CENTRAL GOVERNMENT

INLAND REVENUE
Duties on land values [Domesday Survey] 1910. Volumes covering the Metropolitan Boroughs of Hackney, Shoreditch and Stoke Newington.
Hackney Metropolitan Borough Assessment Committee records:

Minutes 1930-1936, 1940-1950.

Valuation lists 1939-1940.

Shoreditch Metropolitan Borough Assessment Committee records:

Valuation lists 1935-1936.

Stoke Newington Metropolitan Borough Assessment Committee records:

Minutes 1935-1940.

Valuation lists 1934-1935.

ORDNANCE SURVEY
Minor control points albums (boundary area part survey) 1946-1987.

13. RECORDS OF OTHER PUBLIC BODIES

HACKNEY TURNPIKE TRUST
Minutes 1748-1759, 1783-1826.
Roads Committee minutes 1756-1758.
Survey and Special Committee minutes 1821-1825.
Financial records 1771-1826 (gaps).
Record of labour employed 1781-1802.
Record of tolls 1749-1787 (gaps).

HACKNEY POOR LAW UNION
Board of Guardians minutes 1904-1908.
Assessment Committee minutes 1925.
Clerk's accounts 1890-1896.
Agenda papers and returns of out relief 1930.

15. RECORDS OF DIOCESES, ARCHDEACONRIES AND RURAL DEANERIES, CATHEDRALS AND OTHER ECCLESIASTICAL JURISDICTIONS

HACKNEY AND STOKE NEWINGTON RURAL DIACONAL CHAPTER
Minutes 1913-1949.

SHOREDITCH RURAL DEANERY
Minutes 1934-1967.

16. RECORDS OF PARISHES

CHRIST CHURCH CLAPTON
Churchwardens' accounts 1906-1927.
Service register 1920-1931.

GOOD SHEPHERD MISSION, *Falcon Court, Stoke Newington Church Street, Stoke Newington*; **and HOLY REDEEMER MISSION,** *Stoke Newington* **[later ST BARNABAS STOKE NEWINGTON]**
Records 1881-1898.

RAM'S EPISCOPAL CHAPEL, *Homerton*
Trustees minutes 1847-1936.
Annual report 1906-1907.

ST BARNABAS HOMERTON
Vestry minutes 1847-1922.
Collection register 1916-1930.

ST COLUMBIA HAGGERSTON
Service register 1867.

ST JOHN AT HACKNEY
Parish magazines 1915-1944 (gaps).
Plan of churchyard and elevations of surrounding buildings, copy glebe terrier 1618-1633.

ST JOHN OF JERUSALEM SOUTH HACKNEY
Trust document 1810.
Statement of income and expenditure 1827-1829.

ST JOHN THE BAPTIST HOXTON
Election details for churchwardens 1829.

ST JOHN THE EVANGELIST BROWNSWOOD PARK
Records 1939-1988.

ST LEONARD SHOREDITCH
Parish Relief Committee relief books 1904-1911.

ST LUKE HOMERTON
Photographs of the church and incumbents 1886-1972.
Parish magazines 1904-1978 (gaps).
Centenary material 1972.

ST MARK DALSTON
Notes and cuttings 1903-1912.

ST MARY OF ETON HACKNEY WICK
Banns register 1938-1942.

ST MARY STOKE NEWINGTON
Plans of the old and new churches and churchyards c.1885-1916.
Scrapbook on the men's services 1925-1926.
Seat holders records 1882-1884.

ST MARY WITH ST CHAD HAGGERSTON
Parish magazines 1868-1880, 1961-1965 (gaps).

ST MICHAEL SHOREDITCH
Receipts and accounts 1941-1959.

ST THOMAS ARBOUR SQUARE, STEPNEY
St Thomas Institute manuscript magazine 1876-1881.

ST THOMAS UPPER CLAPTON
Stamford Hill and Upper Clapton Provident Society minutes 1855-1905.
Journal of Rev. F. W. Kingsford 1862-1864.
Photographs c.1900-1911.
Copies of the National School's minutes 1828-1890.

WEST HACKNEY CHURCH
Plan of pews and sittings c.1871.

17. RECORDS OF NON-ANGLICAN PLACES OF WORSHIP

17.1 Non-conformist churches

ABNEY CONGREGATIONAL CHAPEL, *Stoke Newington*
Records 1858-1924.

BETHNAL GREEN CIRCUIT
Methodist.
Local preachers' minutes 1878-1896.

BRUCE HALL MISSION, *Hackney*
Methodist.
Church Council minutes 1983-1992.
Leaders' minutes 1946-1963.
Financial records 1927-1951, 1960-1987.
Overseas Mission (Women's Work) records 1948-1982.
Trustee and property records, including plans 1923-1981.

CAMBRIDGE HEATH CONGREGATIONAL CHURCH, *Hackney*
Membership records, including baptisms and marriages 1863-1936 (gaps).
Deacons and Church Meeting minutes 1861-1937.
Building Committee minutes and correspondence 1864-1873.
Trust and property records 1865-1928.

CLAPTON PARK CONGREGATIONAL CHURCH, *Hackney*
Baptisms (as part of minute book) 1907-1941.
Church minutes 1867-1941, 1952-1968.
Deacons' minutes 1873-1962.
Financial records 1871-1924.
Membership records 1879, 1910-1942.
Other records 1793-1965.
Clapton Park Institute minutes and year books 1911-1939.
Clapton Park Literary Society minutes 1891-1914.
Gravel Pit Chapel minutes 1804-1871.
Grove Mission minutes 1905-1925.
Grove Young Men's Institute minutes 1887-1888.
Homerton Chapel Benevolent Society 1793-1989.
Homerton Mission minutes 1886-1887.
Local and National Temperance and Band of Hope records 1880-1972.

CLAPTON PARK METHODIST CHURCH, *Hackney*
Baptism register 1888-1938, 1948-1960.
Leaders' minutes 1962-1979.
Trustees' records 1929-1965.
Annual reports and appeals, including short history 1905-1974.
Pulpit notices and financial records 1928-1983.

CLAPTON WESLEYAN CHURCH [later DOWNS PARK METHODIST CHURCH], *Hackney*
Baptism register 1865-1963.
Leaders' minutes 1876-1892, 1908-1951.
Committee minutes 1865-1916.

Finance Committee minutes 1920-1939.
Trustees' records and minutes 1863-1959.
Pulpit notices and financial records 1865-1970.
Teachers' minutes and Sunday School Council minutes 1902-1913, 1929-1954.
Christian Endeavour Society minutes 1879-1883.
Wesleyan Missionary Society (Clapton Branch) minutes 1916-1960, accounts 1913-1954.

CLAPTON WESLEYAN CIRCUIT, *Hackney*
Methodist.
Quarterly meetings and trust records 1876-1909.

DALSTON CENTRAL MISSION, *Hackney*
Methodist.
Correspondence files on financial matters and premises 1940-1956.

DALSTON CONGREGATIONAL CHURCH, *Hackney*
Minutes, financial records and membership records 1871-1946.

DALSTON METHODIST CHURCH, *Mayfield Road [later Richmond Road], Hackney*
Registers:
        Baptism 1845-1906.
        Marriage 1867-1903.
Leaders' minutes 1929-1956.
Sunday School Council minutes 1924-1964.
Trustees' minutes 1929-1946, 1948-1957, 1971-1976.
Publications and newsletters 1920-1979.

DOWNS BAPTIST CHAPEL, *Hackney*
Minutes, financial records, membership records 1869-1949.

HACKNEY CIRCUIT [later HACKNEY AND VICTORIA PARK CIRCUIT]
Methodist.
Quarterly Meeting minutes, local preachers records and trust records 1887-1931.
Schedules 1927-1937.
First London District minutes 1908-1927.
London Mission Executive Hackney Branch minutes 1925-1952.

HACKNEY AND CLAPTON MISSION CIRCUIT [later HACKNEY MISSION CIRCUIT]
Methodist.
Quarterly minutes 1948-1966.
Schedules and correspondence 1957-1980.

HACKNEY WICK WESLEYAN CHAPEL, *Hackney*
Baptism register 1879-1939.
Trustees' minutes 1888-1915.

HAGGERSTON METHODIST MISSION, *Shoreditch*
Marriage register 1938-1986.

HARBOUR LIGHT METHODIST CHURCH, *Goldsmiths Row, Haggerston, Shoreditch*
Trustees' minutes 1896-1961.

HOMERTON WESLEYAN CHAPEL, *Hackney*; **and CASSLAND ROAD WESLEYAN CHAPEL,** *Hackney*
Marriage register 1885-1889.
Leaders' minutes 1868-1935.
Cassland Road Chapel Trustees' minutes 1949-1956.
Membership records and accounts 1897-1940.
Accounts 1872-1908.

HOXTON ACADEMY CHAPEL, *Shoreditch*
Independent.
Sunday School records 1815-1935.

HOXTON MARKET CHRISTIAN MISSION, *Shoreditch*
Independent.
Annual reports 1914-1919 (gaps).
Appeal, service and other programmes 1917-1983.
Mission magazines 1905-1974.
Photographs 1900-1983.
[See also p.116]

KINGSLAND CONGREGATIONAL CHAPEL, *Dalston, Hackney*
Sunday School Committee minutes 1863-1885.

LATTER RAIN OUTPOURING REVIVAL CHURCH, *Hoxton, Shoreditch*
Independent.
Marriage register 1979-1994.

LOWER CLAPTON CONGREGATIONAL CHURCH, *Hackney*
Registers:
        Baptism 1864-1952.
        Marriage 1864-1952.
Other records 1850-1962.

MABERLY CONGREGATIONAL CHURCH, *Balls Pond Road, Stoke Newington*
Sunday School Committee minutes 1835-1856.

MARE STREET BAPTIST CHAPEL [later FRAMPTON PARK BAPTIST CHURCH], *Hackney*
Marriage register 1934-1944.
Church Meeting minutes 1789-1978.

Deacons' minutes 1894-1979.
Annual reports 1871-1915 (gaps).
Membership records 1789-1988 (including baptisms and burials).
Financial records 1933-1972.
St Ann's Place Sunday School records 1813-1953.
Other records 1854-1984.

NEW GRAVEL PIT CHAPEL, *Hackney*
Unitarian.
General Committee minutes and annual reports 1810-1912
Financial records 1742-1889.
Sunday School Committee minutes 1891-1909.
Sunday School accounts 1790-1811.
Girls School Committee minutes 1820-1832.
Charity School records (boys) 1832-1866.
Unitarian Fellowship Fund minutes 1819-1937.
Other records 1857-1976

NEWINGTON GREEN UNITARIAN CHURCH, *Stoke Newington*
Baptism, marriage and death registers 1841-1889.
Chapel committee minutes 1859-1935.
Trustees' records c.1820-1952.
Membership records 1708-1976.
Annual reports 1878-1958.
Financial records 1854-1965.
Sunday School and School records 1857-1964.
Newington Green Band of Hope minutes and programmes 1893-1907, 1914-1933.
Newington Green Domestic Mission minutes and annual reports 1843-1873.
Newington Green Sunday School Savings Bank and the Penny Savings Bank financial records 1874-1914.
Newington Green Provident Society minutes, reports and financial records 1889-1926.
Newington Green Conversation Society [later Conversation Society and Field Club] minutes and programmes 1848-1907.
Other records 1693-1958.

PACKINGTON STREET METHODIST CHURCH, *Islington*
Trustees' minutes 1930-1968.
Accounts 1931-1965.

PARAGON HALL, *Hackney*
Brethren.
Marriage register 1958-1960.

PEMBURY ROAD UNITED METHODIST FREE CHURCH, *Hackney*
Leaders' and Church Meeting minutes 1901-1927.

POWNALL ROAD CONGREGATIONAL CHURCH, *Shoreditch*
Minutes and membership records 1866-1950.

PRIMITIVE METHODIST CONNEXION CLAPTON CIRCUIT
Methodist.
Quarterly Meetings minutes 1884-1907, 1939-1947.

RECTORY ROAD UNITED REFORMED CHURCH, *Hackney*
Baptism and marriage registers 1887-1933.
Church Meeting minutes 1870-1973.
Deacons' [later Elders'] minutes 1888-1977.
Committee minutes 1889, 1910, 1928-1934.
Membership records 1887-1867.
Hoxton Market Christian Mission Council minutes 1892-1899.
Sunday School Teachers' minutes 1958-1977.
Financial records 1915-1971.
Manuals and newsletters 1883-1968.

RICHMOND ROAD WESLEYAN CHURCH, *Hackney*
Marriage register 1849-1917.

ST THOMAS SQUARE CHAPEL, *Hackney*
Independent.
Registers:
  Baptism 1814-1894.
  Burial 1837-1853.
Deacons' and other committee minutes 1814-1896.
Membership records 1804-1894.
Boys' Sunday School Teachers' minute book 1831-1864.
Financial records 1841-1888.
Property records 1771-1877.

SHRUBLAND ROAD CONGREGATIONAL CHURCH, *Hackney*
Baptism and marriage registers 1913-1966.
Burial registers 1947-1951.
Church Meeting and Deacons' minutes 1878-1968.
Bazaar, Finance and Special Pastorate minutes 1878-1889, 1908-1911.
Sunday School Teachers' minutes 1916-1965.
Financial records 1874-1965.

TRINITY CONGREGATIONAL CHURCH, *South Hackney, Hackney*
Registers:
  Baptism 1852-1975 (commences at Mile End New Town Chapel).
  Marriage 1907-1975.
Church Meeting minutes 1873-1987.
Deacons' Meeting minutes 1892-1988.

Men's Own Society minutes 1906-1922.
Records closed until 30 years old.

UNITED METHODIST FREE CHURCH CIRCUIT
Committee and Local Preachers' records 1877-1939.

VICTORIA PARK CONGREGATIONAL TABERNACLE. *Hackney*
Church Meeting and Deacons' minutes 1869-1901.

20. RECORDS OF ALMSHOUSES

SAMUEL ROBINSON'S CHARITIES: RETREAT AND RELIEF, *Retreat Place, Hackney*
Trustees minutes 1812-1974.
Registers of applications and pensioners 1887-1974.
Trust documents and deeds 1812-1978.

21. RECORDS OF HOSPITALS, ASYLUMS AND DISPENSARIES

BRITISH ASYLUM FOR DEAF AND DUMB FEMALES, *Clapton, Hackney*
Committee minutes 1860-1949.
Annual reports 1856-1947.
Financial records 1858-1941.

STOKE NEWINGTON AND STAMFORD HILL DISPENSARY [formerly THE STAMFORD HILL, STOKE NEWINGTON, CLAPTON, WEST HACKNEY, KINGSLAND AND DALSTON DISPENSARY], *Stoke Newington*
Committee minutes 1843-1930.
Annual reports 1836-1898.
Patient records 1894-1911, 1910-1917.
Subscriptions and accounts 1825-30, 1919-1930.

22. RECORDS OF ORPHANAGES, REFUGES AND PENITENTIARIES

ELIZABETH FRY PROBATION HOSTEL [formerly ELIZABETH FRY REFUGE], Shoreditch
Refuge and Initiating Group minutes 1846-1925, 1938-1953.
Annual reports 1851-1964.
Matron's log and report books 1941-1950, 1952-1956.
Case books c.1849-1955.

FEMALE REFUGE FOR THE DESTITUTE AND MALE REFUGE FOR THE DESTITUTE, *Hackney*
General Court of Governors minutes 1819-1877.
General Committee Female Refuge minutes 1812-1902.
General Committee Male Refuge minutes 1819-1848.
Annual reports 1806-1922.
Case books 1846-1857.

23. RECORDS OF SCHOOLS AND COLLEGES

CLAPTON COUNTY SECONDARY SCHOOL [later JOHN HOWARD SCHOOL], *Hackney*
Accounts 1933-1939.
Log book 1906-1952.
Pupil admission records 1919-1969.
Staff records 1906-1922.
School magazines 1932-1952 (gaps).
Prospectuses 1936, 1973.
Photographs 1931-1932, 1978.

GLYN ROAD EMERGENCY SCHOOL, *Hackney*
Log book 1940-1943.
Admission registers 1940-1941.

GLYN ROAD GIRLS SCHOOL, *Hackney*
Log books, admission registers, attendance registers 1892-1946.

GLYN ROAD WOMEN'S EVENING INSTITUTE [later CLAPTON AND HOMERTON WOMEN'S INSTITUTE; later CLAPTON AND KINGSLAND INSTITUTE], *Hackney*
Log book 1927-1962.

HACKNEY DOWNS SCHOOL [formerly GROCERS' COMPANY SCHOOL], *Hackney*
Admission registers 1876-1907.
Pupil records 1934-1959.
Clove Club [old boys club] 1885-1970.
Headmaster's diaries 1908-1959.
Headmaster's reports to governors 1906-1933, 1962.
H.M. Inspector's reports 1906-1935.
Photographs, including albums 1876-c.1975.
Premises records 1938-1964.
Prospectuses 1882-1913, 1903-1962.
School events, activities and club records, including theatrical programmes 1889-1966.
School magazines 1886-1973 (gaps).
Sporting programmes and records 1894-1964.
Other records 1906-1966.

HOXTON ACADEMY CHAPEL SUNDAY SCHOOL, *Shoreditch*
Committee minutes 1815-1893.
Teachers' meeting minutes 1814-1935.
Cashbooks 1826-1901.
Girls register 1841-1851.

HUTTON POPLARS RESIDENTIAL SCHOOL, *Brentwood, Essex*
Log book 1930-1936.
Plans 1904-1955.
Photographs c.1914-1930.

KINGSLAND SCHOOL [formerly KINGSLAND BIRKBECK SCHOOL; later DALSTON COUNTY SECONDARY SCHOOL], *Hackney*
Correspondence on charitable donations and school war time activity 1914-1918.
Photographs 1914-1970.
School magazines 1914-1960 (gaps).

LAURISTON ROAD JUNIOR MIXED SCHOOL, *Hackney*
Admissions 1945-1956.

NORTH HACKNEY CENTRAL SCHOOL, *Hackney*
Log book 1928-1958.
Pupil records 1928-1951.

RUSHMORE ROAD GIRLS SCHOOL, *Hackney*
Log books and admission registers 1877-1938.

SHOREDITCH CHARITY SCHOOLS, *Shoreditch*
Boys and Girls Schools minutes 1705-1888.
Committee for Building the New Schools minutes 1801-1803.
Annual reports 1838-1875 (gaps).
Subscribers and admissions lists 1828-1881.
Financial records 1705-1898.

STOKE NEWINGTON NATIONAL PAROCHIAL SCHOOL, *Stoke Newington*
Congregation/Managers minutes 1904-1909.
Correspondence 1905-1911.

STOKE NEWINGTON RAGGED SCHOOLS, *Stoke Newington*
Committee minutes 1855-1884.
Accounts 1855-1897.
Reports c.1846-c.1872.

26. RECORDS OF CEMETERIES AND CREMATORIA

ABNEY PARK CEMETERY COMPANY, *Stoke Newington*
Directors' minutes 1850-1879.
Chairman's agenda books 1881-1943 (gaps).
Shareholder records 1899-1964.
Secretary's letter books 1912-1929.
Financial records including annual reports and accounts 1882-1956.
Registers:
      Burial registers 1840-1934, 1936-1978. Indexed.
      Common grave registers 1866-1921 (gaps).
      Private grave registers 1871-1913 (gaps).
      Registers of grave owners and maintenance c.1850-1951 (gaps).
Plans c.1845-1920.
Staff records 1895-1969.
Correspondence 1879-1968.
Records of other cemeteries owned by the company including plans 1905-1980.

28. RECORDS OF MILITARY AND ARMED BODIES

HACKNEY NATIONAL RESERVE
Committee and meeting minutes 1913-1922.
Lists of members 1912-1921.
Correspondence 1912-1921.

HACKNEY VOLUNTEER CORPS
Regulations and signed declarations 1803-1808.

NATIONAL RESERVE FORCE: STOKE NEWINGTON BATTALION
Membership records 1912-1919.
Rules 1914-1915.
Fund raising circulars 1914-1919.
Cuttings 1913-1919.

STOKE NEWINGTON WAR HOSPITAL SUPPLY DEPOT
Minutes 1915-1919.
Production records 1915-1919.
Financial records 1916-1919.
Visitors book 1915-1918.
Correspondence and cuttings 1916-1918.

29. RECORDS OF ASSOCIATIONS, CLUBS AND SOCIETIES

10TH HACKNEY SCOUT GROUP
Accounts of meetings, correspondence and accounts 1950-1956.
Photographic albums of annual camps and activities 1914-1953.

AMALGAMATED ENGINEERING UNION: HACKNEY BRANCH
Membership records 1896-c.1970.

AMALGAMATED ENGINEERING UNION: STOKE NEWINGTON BRANCH
Minutes 1925-1967 (gaps).

AMALGAMATED SOCIETY OF UPHOLSTERERS: LONDON NO. 1 BRANCH
Minutes 1891-1947.
Financial records 1889-1940.
Membership records 1889-1906.
Out of work books 1939-1947.

AMALGAMATED SOCIETY OF WOODWORKERS: HACKNEY 2ND BRANCH
Minutes 1952-1960.
Financial record 1945-1956.
Membership records 1945-1954.
Secretary's letter books 1949-1953.

ASSOCIATION FOR THE BETTER GOVERNMENT OF THE PARISH OF ST JOHN AT HACKNEY
Minutes 1861-1863.

BOROUGH OF STOKE NEWINGTON RATEPAYERS AND ELECTORS ASSOCIATION
Minutes and annual reports 1900-1933.

BRITISH LADIES SOCIETY FOR PROMOTING THE REFORMATION OF FEMALE PRISONERS
Minutes and annual reports 1821-1891.

BRITISH WOMEN'S TEMPERANCE ASSOCIATION: STOKE NEWINGTON BRANCH
Committee minutes and agendas 1908-1918.
Subscribers 1890-1900.
Annual reports 1881-1900.

CHARITY OF CRANSTON AND MARSHALL
Cranston's Trustees' minutes 1880-1887.
Marshall's Trustees' minutes 1887-1983.
Trustees' attendance register 1907-1984.
Correspondence applications and agendas 1964-1983.
Closed until thirty years old.

CONSERVATIVE ASSOCIATION: BOROUGH OF HACKNEY CENTRAL DIVISION
Minutes 1885-1899.

DE BEAUVOIR ASSOCIATION
Records of public enquiry into De Beauvoir Southern area 1971-1985.

ELECTRICAL TRADES UNION: HACKNEY BRANCH
Minutes 1941-1959.
Membership records 1946-1965.

ELECTRICAL TRADES UNION: BETHNAL GREEN BRANCH
Minutes 1952-1962.
Membership records 1949-1959.

GIRLS GUILD OF THE GOOD LIFE
Annual reports 1892-1953 (gaps).
Financial records 1843-1971.
Subscriptions 1881-1923 (gaps).

HACKNEY DAY NURSERY
Attendance registers 1934-1935, 1941-1942.
Annual reports 1934-1944.
Other records 1939-1944.

HACKNEY DISTRICT NATIONAL RELIEF FUND
Minute book 1914-1917.

HACKNEY LITERARY AND SCIENTIFIC INSTITUTION
Reports and programmes of lectures and activities of the institute 1853-1872.

HACKNEY PHOTOGRAPHIC SOCIETY
Council and other minutes 1894-1983.
Membership and accounting records 1892-1982.
Photographs 1889-1978.
Certificates, printed books and lantern slide projector 1858-1905.

HACKNEY SOCIAL WORKERS' GROUP [formerly HACKNEY AND STOKE NEWINGTON SOCIAL WORKERS' GROUP]
Committee minutes, general minutes and annual reports 1941-1968.
Membership lists 1970-1973.
Financial records 1962-1976.
Hackney Social Workers News 1970-1972.

HACKNEY SOUTH AND SHOREDITCH LABOUR PARTY
Papers of member 1977-1981. *Closed until 30 years old.*

HACKNEY TEACHERS ASSOCIATION
Minutes 1909-1969 (gaps).

HORNSEY PAROCHIAL CHARITIES
Charity register accounts 1929-1939.

JOINT INDUSTRIAL COUNCIL FOR MANUAL WORKERS NON TRADING SERVICES: LONDON DISTRICT
Minutes 1923-1928, 1944-1949.

LEAGUE OF FRIENDS OF HACKNEY HOSPITAL [later HACKNEY AND HOMERTON HOSPITALS]
Records 1961-1979.

LEAGUE OF FRIENDS OF ST JOHN'S HOSPITAL FOR DISEASES OF THE SKIN
Records 1985-1988.

LEAGUE OF FRIENDS OF THE EASTERN HOSPITAL
Records 1954-1988.

LITERARY READING SOCIETY, *Stoke Newington*
Minutes 1894-1897, 1902-1920.

LONDON JOINT COUNCIL: MANUAL WORKERS
General Purposes Committee minutes 1955-1960.

LONDON LADIES TAILORS, MACHINISTS AND PRESSERS TRADE UNION
Financial records 1913-1921.

LUBAVITCH FOUNDATION
Programmes and magazines 1959-1985.

NATIONAL AMALGAMATED FURNISHING TRADES ASSOCIATION
Minutes 1937-1944.
Financial records 1939-1940.
Correspondence 1946-1972.

NATIONAL AND LOCAL GOVERNMENT OFFICERS ASSOCIATION: STOKE NEWINGTON BRANCH [formerly THE STOKE NEWINGTON MUNICIPAL OFFICERS ASSOCIATION]
Minutes 1914-1936, 1940-1964.
Committee minutes 1935-1948, 1957.

NATIONAL UNION OF TAILORS AND GARMENT WORKERS: LONDON MANTLE AND COSTUME BRANCH
Minutes 1939-1955.
Financial records 1947-1951.
Membership records 1939-1951.

NORTH LONDON ANTIQUARIAN SOCIETY
Proceedings 1906-1922.

NORTH LONDON CHESS CLUB
Committee minutes 1876-1929.
Financial records 1875-1923.
Reports 1880-1923.
Fixtures and associated correspondence 1893-1929.

OLD GRAVEL PIT SICK AND PROVIDENT SOCIETY
Annual reports and balance sheets 1897-1966.

ST JOSEPH'S BURIAL SOCIETY
Collector's book 1865-1869.

SHOREDITCH AND FINSBURY LABOUR PARTY
Minutes 1948-1970.
Accounts 1958-1961.
Correspondence 1948-1954.

SOCIALIST HEALTH ASSOCIATION: EAST LONDON BRANCH
Minutes 1988-1990.

STOKE NEWINGTON LITERARY AND SCIENTIFIC ASSOCIATION
Minutes 1888-1938.

STOKE NEWINGTON RATEPAYERS ASSOCIATION
Minutes 1884-1894.
Membership records 1886-1890.

SUN BABIES NURSERY, *Shoreditch*
Trustees' minutes 1941-1963.
Attendance register 1942-1950.

UNITED LADIES TAILORS TRADE UNION
Committee minutes 1922-1939.
Financial records 1919-1939.

UNISON NO. 1 BRANCH EC [formerly NATIONAL AND LOCAL GOVERNMENT OFFICERS ASSOCIATION: LONDON BOROUGH OF HACKNEY BRANCH]
Minutes and presented papers 1968-1996.

WOMENS' NATIONAL CANCER CONTROL CAMPAIGN: HACKNEY AND DISTRICT BRANCH
Minutes, cuttings and correspondence 1964-1988.

WORKERS CIRCLE FRIENDLY SOCIETY
Central Committee and branch minutes 1940-1980.
Financial records 1958-1985.
Membership records 1912-1984.
Administration of rest home records 1958-1975.
Other records 1934-1968.

30. RECORDS OF THEATRES AND CINEMAS

HACKNEY EMPIRE THEATRE, *Mare Street, Hackney*
Contracts and site purchase documents 1896-1962.
Theatre posters 1986-c.1994.

31. RECORDS OF BUSINESS ASSOCIATIONS AND MARKET EXCHANGES

BRITISH MATCH MAKERS ASSOCIATION
Meeting minutes 1903-1909.
Advisory committee meeting minutes 1903-1905.

HACKNEY TRADES COUNCIL
Minutes 1900-1907, 1952-1966, 1968-1994.
Committee and sub-committee minutes 1953-1977.
Financial and membership records 1952-1987.
Secretary's correspondence 1952-1987.
Correspondence on the Defence Fund and legal case involving Horatio Bottomley 1903-1909.
Photographs c.1920-1956.

JOINT INDUSTRIAL COUNCIL FOR THE MATCH MANUFACTURING INDUSTRY
London District Council minutes 1919-1922.
Other records 1926-1959.

SOCIETY OF BRITISH MATCH MANUFACTURERS
Accounts with correspondence 1918-1950.
Reports 1953-1959.
Correspondence 1947-1960.

UNITED KINGDOM MATCH MAKERS ASSOCIATION
Minutes 1872-1878.

33. RECORDS OF BUSINESSES

A. CALTON AND SON LTD, *De Beauvoir Road, Hackney*
Bakers.
Records 1937-1965.

A. NORMAN AND SONS LTD, *Shoreditch*
Footwear wholesalers.
Directors' reports and accounting records 1948-1971.
Articles of association and prospectuses 1906-1973.
Correspondence on takeovers and mergers1964-1973.
Financial records 1936-1973.
Staffing records 1941-1960.

A. SINDALL AND CO., *Hackney Road, Hackney; Dalston, Hackney*
Trimming manufacturers.
Collected records and photographs 1868-1981.
Correspondence 1920-1980.
Executors' papers for G. B. Sindall's estate 1914-1930.
Factory registers 1902-1938.
Partnership records of premises in Albion and Malvern Road 1921-1952.
Samples and ephemera 1909-1976.

BATEY AND CO., *Shoreditch*
Drinks manufacturers.
Reports of directors, balance sheets, stock records 1941-1952.

BERGER, JENSON AND NICHOLSON [formerly LEWIS BERGER AND SONS], *Homerton, Hackney*
Paint manufacturers.
Directors' minutes 1879-1967.
Accounts 1802-1810, 1883-1935.
Advertising and public relations records 1914-1984.
Company histories 1898-1984.
Corporate records 1950-1984.
Letter books 1881-1945.
Production records 1815-1978.
Property and premises records 1717-1861, 1878-1981.
Reports 1960-1985.
Sales and Letter books 1778-1843, 1881-1897.
Staff records 1831, 1868-1897, 1926-1984.

Other records 1773-1986.

Records of associated companies:

Allen Davis (Wallpapers) Ltd. 1967-1984.

Barnes and Sons [previously Ross Co. (Leeds) Ltd]. 1913-1983.

Berger Traffic Markings Ltd. 1947-1972.

Bristow, Wadley and Co. Ltd. 1954-1983.

British Paints Ltd. 1949-1982.

C. Clifford Ltd. 1954, 1960-1984.

Cardiff Glazing and Mirror Products Ltd. 1946-1951.

Colorbrush Ltd. 1925-1960.

Direct Paints Ltd. 1970-1984.

Ernest Hunter (Coxhoe) Ltd. 1945-1983.

Frank Hart and Co. Ltd. 1946-1984.

G. Widger and Sons Ltd. 1952-1983.

H. Chapell and Co. (Est. 1934) Ltd. 1930-1965.

H.C. Hitchman Ltd. 1938-1952.

Harker, Sanders Ltd. 1947-1984.

J.M. Seed (Preston) Ltd. 1973-1984.

Jenson and Nicholson. 1859-1986.

John Carter (Paints) Ltd. 1953-1984.

John Hall and Sons (Bristol) Ltd. 1797-1973.

John Hunter Wallpaper Stores Ltd. 1971-1984.

Keystone Paint and Varnish Co. Ltd. 1941-1959.

Lewis Berger and Sons of America Ltd. 1899-1900.

Lewis Berger and Sons (Australia) Pty. Ltd. 1911-1937.

Lewis Berger and Sons (New Zealand) Ltd. 1931-1937.

Lewis Berger and Sons (South Africa) Ltd. 1921-1937.

Lindsley Wallpaper and Hardware Stores Ltd. 1947-1959.

MacGregor Wallcoverings Ltd. 1964-1977.

Matex Ltd. 1920-1970.

P.G.W. Holdings Ltd. 1966-1972.

P.J. Mott Gotobed Co. Ltd. 1961-1983.

P.M. Walker Ltd. 1924-1939.

Pickels Garden Products Ltd [formerly Pickles (Paints) Ltd]. 1966-1984.

Ruddlesdens Ltd. 1966-1984

Schmidt, Conrad W. 1877-1907.

Sherwin-Williams (Ireland) Ltd. 1935-1938.

Sherwin-Williams Co. (New Zealand) Ltd. 1935-1937.

Sissons Paints (Eastern) Ltd. 1957.

Spelthorne Metals Ltd. 1925-1956.

Topdec Ltd. 1960-1984.

Trend Ltd. 1969-1984.

Varden Laboratories Ltd. 1941-1984.

W. Symonds Ltd. 1931-1964.

W.A. Rose and Co. Ltd. 1917-1948.

Waitell Wallpapers Ltd. 1946-1983.

Western Wallpapers Ltd. 1946-1966.
Wylie's Cleaners [later Berger Group Supplies]. 1910-1978.

BRIGGS, Thomas, *Southgate Road, Hackney*
Tentmakers.
Catalogues and photographs of premises c.1900-1970.

BRITISH XYLONITE CO. LTD, *Homerton, Hackney; Walthamstow, Essex; Brantham, Suffolk*
Plastic manufacturers.
Directors, shareholders and general minutes 1877-1925.
Balance sheets and directors reports 1918-1954 (gaps).
Correspondence concerning visit to Formosa and Japan 1897-1901.
Financial and production records 1877-1939.
Plant records 1893-1917.
Premises records 1877-1917.
Production records 1886-1939.
Share records 1877-1930.
Stocktaking records 1908-1930.
Records of associated companies:
  British Tortelloid Ltd. 1932-1938.
  British Xylonite (Australia) Proprietary Ltd. 1931-1950.
  British Xylonite (Canada) Ltd. 1922-1939.
  British Xylonite Co. New York Inc. 1914-1927.
  British Xylonite Co. Vienna, Austria. 1908-1914.
  Cascelloid Ltd. 1931-1955.
  Daniel Spill and Co. Ltd. c.1880.
  Homerton Manufacturing Co. Ltd. 1877-1910.
  The Xylonite Company. 1869-1877.

BRYANT AND MAY LTD, *Fairfield Works, Bow, Poplar; Liverpool; Glasgow*
Match manufacturers.
Directors meeting minutes 1884-1947.
General meeting minutes 1884-1960.
Stockholders meeting minutes 1913-1945.
Executive committee meeting minutes 1919-1927.
Annual reports and accounts 1884-1963.
Financial records 1852-1882, 1884-1977.
Advertising material 1865-c.1970.
Book match label proofs and order books 1905-1975.
Catalogues and price lists 1872-1940.
Correspondence 1870-1974.
Estate records 1920-1968.
House magazine 1921-1968.
Newspaper cuttings 1902-1973.
Patent records 1855-1933.
Premises papers 1893-1959.

Production records 1856-1956.

Public relations records c.1930s-1972.

Records of Francis May, founder, 1827-1880.

Share records 1884-1939.

Staffing records 1852-1960. *Closed for up to 75 years.*

Trade mark registers 1876-1979.

Travellers circular letters, price lists and papers 1901-1959.

Brymay Athletic Association records 1900-1966.

Records of associated companies:

 Acton Match Co. Ltd. 1924-1963.

 Alliance Match Co. Ltd. 1932-1964.

 Bell and Black Match Co. Ltd. 1876-1881.

 British Basket and Besto Co. Ltd. 1933-1970.

 British Booklet Matches (1928) Ltd. 1928-1961.

 British Match Corporation [holding company which owned Bryant and May 1927-1974]. 1927-1974.

 Bryant and May, Bell and Co. (Pty) Ltd, Australia. 1909-1960.

 Bryant and May, Bell and Co. (Pty) Ltd, New Zealand. 1909-1949.

 Bryant and May (Forestry) Ltd. 1961-1970.

 Brymay Partnership Trust Ltd records 1920-1961.

 Brymay Savings Bank records 1948-1972.

 Diamond Match Co. Ltd. 1897-1963.

 Dixon, Son and Evans. 1877-1886.

 F. Gough and Son Ltd. 1933-1970.

 Federal Match Co. Ltd. 1920-1967.

 Hulme Patent Advertising Match Co. Ltd. 1936-1960.

 Irish Match Co. Ltd. 1897-1967.

 Jahncke Ltd. 1878-1960.

 J. and G. Cox Ltd. 1898-1975.

 Lion Match Co. Ltd. 1905-1962.

 Maguire, Paterson and Palmer Ltd. 1919-1963.

 Matches Ltd. 1913-1965.

 Motormaps Ltd. 1953-1967.

 Octavius Hunt Ltd. 1928-1941.

 Print and Paper Ltd. 1954-1971.

 Printpack Ltd. 1958-1967.

 R. Bell and Co. Ltd. 1887-1963.

 S.J. Moreland and Sons Ltd. 1917-1972.

 Standard Match Co. Ltd. 1931-1966.

 Swedish Match Co. 1877-1959.

 Thomas Nimmo and Co. Ltd. 1852-1959.

 W.J. Morgan and Co. Ltd. 1883-1964.

 Western Australia Match Co. Ltd. 1930-1950.

 Wilkinson Match Ltd [holding company which owned Bryant and May 1974-1978]. 1974-1978.

Records of Government bodies:

 Match Control Office 1917-1919.

BUNCH AND DUKE, *Hackney*
Estate agents.
Photographs of properties sold 1984-1985.

C.F. CASELLA AND CO. LTD, *Holborn; Britannia Walk, Shoreditch*
Instrument makers.
Stock books 1862-1912.
Order books 1883-1963.
Other records 1855-1960.

CARLESS, CAPEL AND LEONARD LTD, *Hackney Wick, Hackney*
Refiners and distillers of oil.
Company magazines and history files 1901-1989.
Photographs c.1890-1987.
Press cuttings 1962-1988.
Production and stock records 1933-1952.
Sales records 1912-1949.
Title deeds and site plans 1860-1974.

DOTTERIDGE BROTHERS LTD, *East Road, Shoreditch*
Funeral equipment manufacturers.
Financial records 1939-1964.
Records of associated companies:
      Dotteridge School for Embalming and Funeral Hygiene. 1896-1971.
      Other companies. 1925-1976.

F. PUCKERIDGE AND NEPHEW LTD, *Upper Clapton Road, Hackney*
Goldbeaters, skins and moulds manufacturers.
Out letter books 1892-1920.
Purchase day book 1936-1950.

FOX Family, *Hackney*
Builders and developers.
Deeds and business correspondence 1743-1927.

GARDNER AND GARDNER, *Wapping; De Beauvoir Road, Hackney*
Corn merchants.
Accounting records 1963-1967.
Customer ledger 1937-1951.

GLOVERS (DYERS AND CLEANERS) LTD, *Lower Clapton, Hackney*
Directors' minutes 1945-1984.
Accounts 1964-1984.
Property records 1935-1980.
Closed until 30 years old.

HACKNEY GAZETTE, *Hackney*
Newspaper.
Photographers diaries and negatives 1983-1993.
Scrapbook with cuttings of photos 1974-1978.

HARPER, William, *Shoreditch*
Bookseller.
Catalogues, book orders and photographs and correspondence 1856-1903.

HILDESELY, Henry, *Shacklewell, Hackney*
Printers.
Ephemera and cuttings 1932-1940.

J. AND W. NICHOLSON AND CO. LTD, *Clerkenwell; Three Mills, Bow, Poplar*
Distillers.
Accounting records 1872-1969.
Employee and staff records 1852-1873, 1878-1913, 1967-1968.
Estate records 1760-1916.
Family records 1597-1950.
Letter books 1900-1930.
Loans records (to publicans) 1832-1905.
Partnership records1763-1892, 1969.
Premises records 1872-1893,1935-1947.
Production and stock records 1840-1951.
Sales and customer records 1808-1956.
Records of associated companies:
       P. D. Carnegie and Sons. 1950-1956.
       Reid Wright and Holloway. 1905-1942.
       Three Mills Bonded Warehouses Ltd. 1951-1958.

JAQUIN, C.A. [later JAQUIN, C.J.], *Shoreditch*
Button makers.
Records 1829-1902.

JAMES RECKNALL AND CO., *Hackney*
Undertakers.
Accounts 1886-1970.

JOHN CARTER AND SONS LTD, *Kingsland Road, Shoreditch*
Boot and shoe makers.
Directors and shareholders minutes 1896-1970.
Correspondence and agreements 1879-1937.
Sales and production records 1862-1878, 1897-1898, 1956, 1967-1973.
Share records 1897-1918, 1951-1965.
Wages and pension records 1887-1946.

Records of associated companies:
Dorman and Co. Ltd. 1920-1958.
John Carter and Lindrea (Leathers) Ltd. 1960-1973.
Lindrea and Co. Ltd of Bristol. 1927-1970.
Thomas Walker Ltd. 1924-1972.

L.I. ROSENTHAL AND CO., *Shoreditch*
Boot makers.
Financial statements 1935-1938.

LATHAM, James, *Shoreditch*
Timber and hardwood importers.
Trade catalogues 1935-1937.

LONDON AND SUBURBAN LAND AND BUILDING CO. LTD, *Buckingham Street, Westminster*
Estate development association.
Directors rough minutes 1894-1919.
Board agendas 1914-1924.
Share and dividend records 1863-1923.
Accounting records 1883-1954.

LONDON LANE SHOES LTD, *London Lane, Hackney*
Shoe manufacturers.
Records 1973-1982.

MAGUIRE AND PATERSON LTD, *Dublin, Ireland; London; Liverpool; Belfast, Northern Ireland; Canada*
Match makers.
Financial records 1916-1932.
Correspondence 1920-1933.

MARLA LTD, *Mare Street, Hackney*
Women's clothes manufacturer.
Accounting records 1927-1966.
Scrapbook 1937-1977.

PHINEAS FREEDMAN AND CO. LTD, *Shoreditch*
Furniture warehousemen.
Correspondence concerning insurance and a fire 1885-1887.

PLANET BENEFIT BUILDING AND INVESTMENT SOCIETY, *Hackney*
Trustee records 1869-1874.

PRINGLE, Robert, *Brick Lane, Spitalfields, Bethnal Green*
Pewterers.
Customer ledgers 1866-1872, 1911-1913.

RICHARD ELLIS AND SON, *Hackney*
Surveyors.
Reports on local buildings 1896-1927.

RICHARD PYE AND SONS LTD, *Finsbury; Shoreditch*
Box makers.
Minutes of directors and shareholders meetings 1952-1960.
Accounting records 1883-1960.
Deeds of properties in Shoreditch 1806-1953.
Premises records 1914-1953.
Cuttings books and other associated records 1947-1953.
Photographs and drawings of staff 1945-1954.
Records of associated companies:
       British Nameloid Products Ltd. 1951-1958.
       British Paper Box Federation. 1948-1959.
       Transparent Packing Manufacturing Co. Ltd. 1958-1961.
       Westland Cartons Ltd. 1961-1962.

ROWLEY, Charles, *Shoreditch*
Veneer panel maker.
Accounts 1945-1955.

SEVAK, Lewis, *Dalston, Hackney*
Photographer.
Wedding and studio photographs 1921-1940.

SNEWIN'S DAIRY, *Upper Clapton, Hackney*
Bank book 1905-1909.
Photographs of premises c.1920.

VICTORY ENGINEERS, *Stoke Newington Church Street, Stoke Newington; Milton Keynes*
Reamer manufacturers.
Accounting and sales records 1942-1978.
Patent for reamers 1953.
Agreements for machine hire and insurance 1962-1976.

WILLIAM BAILEY AND SON [later BAILEY AND SLOPER], *Shoreditch*
Furniture and looking glass makers.
Records 1808-1922.

34. FAMILY AND PERSONAL PAPERS AND RECORDS OF PRIVATE ESTATES

AMHERST Family, *Hackney*
Estate and family records of William Amhurst Tyssen Amherst, 1st Baron Amherst of Hackney.
Accounting records and rentals for the Hackney estate 1855-1919.
Archaeological research on Egyptian, Babylonian and other topics 1863-1899.
Correspondence 1840-1901.
Estate papers 1639-1960.
Estate papers concerning property in France 1882-1907.
Parliamentary papers c.1890-1915.
Printed ephemera 1673-1900.
Records concerning the family's origin in Holland 1611-1876.

AUKLAND Family, *Cazenove Road, Stoke Newington*
Shipping papers, family history and ephemera 1865-1922.

BRADLAUGH, Charles (1833-1891), *Hackney*
Freethinker and M.P.
Correspondence concerning Bramlaugh's support for home rule in India, pamphlets and biographical material c.1900-1983.

BROWN, T.E., *Hackney*
Air raid precaution diaries, photographs and other papers 1939-1945.

BURTON, John Francis, *Stoke Newington*
Literary works 1915-1940.

DAWSON, John, *Hoxton Market, Shoreditch*
Excise man and book collector.
Catalogue of book collection 1730-1765.
Diary 1722-1741.

DOBREE, Samuel
Personal papers relating to Hackney Association for the Preservation of Peace, Liberty and Property and Hackney Volunteers 1792-1820.

HARRIS Family, *Clapton, Hackney; Homerton, Hackney*
Family and merchant shipping papers 1855-1904.

HARDY, Charles Ferderick, *Stoke Newington*
Holiday and travel diaries England and Europe 1880-1927.
Family memoirs and letters 1906-1928.

JASPER, A.F.
Author.
Texts of articles and books on his childhood and youth in Hoxton and Walthamstow 1968.

JONES, W.F. Fenton, *Hackney*
Mayor of Hackney 1910-1911.
Cuttings books 1910-1932.

LEASK Family, *Hackney; Stoke Newington*
Programmes of entertainments in Hackney and Stoke Newington 1905-1930, 1963-1964.
Photographs of local churches, Members of Parliament and clergy 1904-1963.

LODDIGES Family, *Hackney*
Nurserymen.
Family papers 1757-1882.

LOWETH Family, *Hackney*
Scrapbook including local Conservative Association material 1910-1954.
Autobiography of Colonel W.E. Loweth c.1960.

MADDISON Family, *Hackney*
Reminiscences of J. Maddison of First World War 1914-1918.
Photographs 1905-1910.

MUDIE and STEWART Families, *Shoreditch*
Family papers 1849-1889.

NORRIS Family, *South Hackney, Hackney*
Estate records 1652-1805, 1843-1919, 1924-1958.
Church construction records 1848-1867.
South Hackney charities records 1838-1852.

PEARSON Estate, *Hoxton, Shoreditch*
Deeds 1615-1957.
Rental books 1830-1933.

RAWLINGS, W.J.
Personal papers relating to River Lea rowing clubs 1909-1939.

RHODES SETTLED ESTATES, *Dalston, Hackney; Hampstead*
Property, sale and development records, Lamb Farm Estate and part later called Dalston Estate 1789-1983.
Accounts, plans and correspondence relating to Dalston and Hampstead estates 1908-1946.

RUSTON Family
Personal notes and photographs especially relating to Hackney Downs School and Newington Green Unitarian Church 1959-1995.

STANTON, *Councillor* **John,** *Stoke Newington*
Political papers 1946-1971.
Family papers 1940-1964.
Hornsey Poor Allotments Charity accounts 1954-1955.

TYRRELL, Roger, *Hackney*
Labour party papers, including material for South Hackney, Shoreditch and Haggerston wards 1972-1981.
Closed until thirty years old.

WHITE, F.H., *Hackney*
Family and political papers relating to Hackney Labour Party, Southwold Ward, 1906-1952.

WILKINSON, *Rev.* **Watts,** *Shoreditch*
Chaplain of Aske's Hospital, Hoxton.
Correspondence 1778-1791.

WOOD, A. Stanley
Agapemonite Church, Clapton, records 1858-1907.

YATES, C. Fisher
Personal papers relating to his time as Mayor of Hackney 1933-1934, and cuttings and correspondence concerning Disabled Soldiers and Sailors (Hackney) Foundation 1918-1945.

ZEALL and SMITH Families, *Hackney*
Family and estate papers 1847-1935.

35. MANORIAL RECORDS

HOXTON, *Shoreditch*
Notice of Court Baron 1823.

KINGSHOLD, *Hackney*
Value of the manor 1704.
Quit rentals 1705-1906, 1712, 1782.
Conveyance of the manor 1814.

LORDSHOLD, *Hackney*
Value of the manor 1704.
Conveyance of the manor 1696.

STEPNEY AND HACKNEY
Agreement on customs and list of tenants 1617-1623.
Conveyance of the manor 1550.

STOKE NEWINGTON
Title deeds of the lessees of the manor 1766-1821.
Copies of court roll 1548-1565.

WENLOCKSBARN, *Finsbury and Shoreditch*
Lease of the manor 1777.

37. ANTIQUARIANS' COLLECTIONS

37.2 Other collections

BAGUST, Florence
Historian.
5 volumes of notes, copy items and cuttings relating to Hackney especially Clapton, compiled c.1913-1929.
Notes on postal history, local churches, Hackney School, Newcome's Scrapbook of North London Antiquarian Society 1906-1910.

BAXTER, Wynne E. and F.W.
Antiquarians.
Notes on Stoke Newington clergy, street names and working notes of transcripts of monuments c.1920-c.1930.
Obituary and biographical material 1863-1923.

MARCHAM, W. McB. (fl.1931-1934)
Abstracts and copies of court rolls for the manor of Stoke Newington 1569-1832.

RENSON, Israel (1906-1986)
Chemist and local historian.
Publications and research notes on Hackney and Victoria Park c.1930-1985.
Family correspondence and photographs c.1930s-1980.
Lantern slide collection of London subjects 1920s-1930s.
Business records 1925-1959.

ROBINSON, William
Antiquarian and local historian.
Correspondence to John Nicholls and others on local history 1840-1843.

SAGE, E.J.
Antiquarian.
Correspondence, articles, extracts and notes on Stoke Newington history c.1860-1891.
Transcripts of the registers of St Mary Stoke Newington 1559-1835.

SHIRREN, A.J.
Local historian.
Articles and texts on Stoke Newington literary and historical subjects compiled mid 20th century.

SPRATLING, J.R. (1854-1934)
Antiquarian and editor.
Research notes on Stoke Newington c.1900-1925.
Articles and ephemera relating to Rams Episcopal Chapel, Homerton, Hackney, 1872-1879.
Articles, fiction and cuttings c.1880-1927.

TYSSEN, J.F.R.
The Tyssen library formed the basis of the Hackney Metropolitan Borough local history collection, having its origins in the collections of the Tyssen family, Lords of the Manors of Hackney, Kingshold and Lordshold.
Antiquarian notes and papers c.1850-1884.
Printed ephemera, especially relating to Hackney Societies c.1750-1850.
Transcripts of Hackney parish and other records 1671-1870.
Copies of estate maps from 1765 and 1785 showing Tyssen properties.
Street plan of Hackney and Stoke Newington, showing sewers 1856.
Plan of Lamb Farm Estate c.1850.

38. COPIES OF SOURCE MATERIAL HELD ELSEWHERE

ALLEN, Henry Robert
Builder.
Notebook, including antiquarian notes c.1868-1872.
[Original in private collection]

BOLTON, John, *Hoxton, Shoreditch*
Diary 1857.

BUTTERS Family
Family papers c.1890-1910.
[Originals in private collection]

CLARKE, NICHOLLS AND COOMBES [later CLARNICO], *Hackney*
Confectionery makers.
Premises plans 1948.
[Originals in private collection]

DALSTON INFANT ASYLUM
Committee minutes 1827-1849.
Annual reports 1831-1934.

NATIONAL UNION OF SHEET METAL WORKERS, COPPERSMITH, HEATING AND DOMESTIC ENGINEERS
Committee minutes 1904-1905.
[Originals in private collection]

S.J. MORELAND AND SONS LTD
Board and shareholder meeting minutes 1917-1951.

SOUP SOCIETY FOR HACKNEY, HOMERTON AND CLAPTON
Annual report 1867.
[Original in private collection]

SPILLER, James
Architect.
Correspondence and plans for new church for St John at Hackney 1791-1820.
[Originals in private collection]

Franco-British Exhibition, White City, 1908

London Borough of Hammersmith and Fulham

Hammersmith and Fulham Archives and Local History Centre
The Lilla Huset
191 Talgarth Road
London
W6 8BJ

Tel:
020-8741 5159
020-8753 3850

Fax:
020-8741 4882

E-mail:
archives@lbhf.gov.uk

Website:
www.lbhf.gov.uk

Location:
In Lilla Huset, 191 Talgarth Road.
Disabled access.

Nearest stations:
Hammersmith (District, Piccadilly and Hammersmith and City Lines). 200 metres.

Parking:
No car parking available (except disabled by prior notice). Public car parks and metered parking in Hammersmith.

Days of opening:
Monday, Tuesday, Thursday and one Saturday a month.

Administrative history:
The London Borough of Hammersmith and Fulham comprises the former Metropolitan Boroughs of Fulham and Hammersmith. Both were in the County of Middlesex before 1889 and in the County of London 1889-1965.

Although Hammersmith was part of the ancient parish of Fulham until 1834, Hammersmith Vestry was responsible for the administration of the Hammersmith part of the parish from the early 17th century.

The Fulham District Board of Works was created in 1855 and covered both Fulham and Hammersmith parishes until it was abolished in 1886.

From 1837 to 1845 the parishes of Fulham and Hammersmith were part of the Kensington Poor Law Union. In 1845 the two parishes united to form the Fulham Union. This was dissolved in 1899 and the parishes became the separate unions of Fulham and Hammersmith until 1930.

Holdings:

The Archives and Local History Centre opened in 1992 and amalgamated the holdings of the Archives Department at Shepherds Bush Library, the Fulham Local Collection at Fulham Library and the Hammersmith Local Collection at Hammersmith Library.

Catalogues and indexes:

Catalogues being converted into an electronic database.

General card index for the archive collections; includes entries for personal names, place, subject and enquiries.

Separate author, title, subject, biographical, street names and classified indexes covering the Fulham and Hammersmith Local Collections.

Slide collection index.

Lists of many of the record groups in the archive collection.

Postal and telephone enquiries:

Staff will undertake short searches for enquirers.

Answering machine for messages when staff not available.

Services:

Photographic service; reproduction fees charged when appropriate.

Photocopying facilities; staff-operated. Original or fragile material may not be photocopied.

Microform reader/printers.

Talks; fees charged.

Publications, reproduction maps, postcards and greetings cards on sale; list available.

Related collections held elsewhere:

LEIGHTON HOUSE ART GALLERY AND MUSEUM
12 Holland Park Road
London
W14 8LZ
(tel: 020-7602 3316)
Holds the Cecil French Bequest on loan; see p. 148.

MUSEUM OF FULHAM PALACE
Bishops Avenue
London
SW6 6EA
(tel: 020-7736 3233)

Museum collection and published material relating to Fulham Palace and the Bishops of London.

1. BOOKS, PAMPHLETS AND PERIODICALS

Wide range of books and pamphlets on the history of Fulham and Hammersmith and its residents. All publications relating to the borough, past and present are purchased where possible.

Periodicals published by local churches, schools, tenants' and residents' associations, history societies, amenity and pressure groups, pensioners' groups, local firms, estate agents etc.

Selected books:
FERET, C. J., *Fulham old and new* (1900).
WHITTING, P.D. ed., *A history of Hammersmith* (1965).

2. SPECIAL COLLECTIONS OF PRINTED MATERIAL

A. P. HERBERT COLLECTION
Books by Sir Alan P. Herbert.

DOVES PRESS AND ERAGNY PRESS COLLECTION
Some Doves Press and Eragny Press books.

KELMSCOTT PRESS COLLECTION
Complete set of Kelmscott Press books.

THEATRE PROGRAMMES COLLECTION
Programmes for the King's Theatre, Lyric Theatre and Shepherds Bush Empire, Hammersmith. A few programmes for the Grand and Granville Theatres, Fulham.

WHITE CITY EXHIBITIONS COLLECTION
Books, programmes, newspaper cuttings, photographs etc. on exhibitions held at the White City 1908-1914. Also includes material relating to the 1908 Olympic Games held at the White City.

WILLIAM MORRIS COLLECTION
Books, pamphlets, cuttings, photographs etc. by and about William Morris. Includes items from collection of Henry Buxton Foreman (1842-1917), editor and bibliographer. Also includes a small collection of fabrics and wallpapers designed by Morris and some personal items such as his pipe and spectacles.

3. NEWSPAPERS

WEST LONDON OBSERVER 1855-1984 (gaps); continued as WEST LONDON LEADER 1984-1987; continued as HAMMERSMITH AND CHISWICK LEADER 1987-1988; continued as HAMMERSMITH AND FULHAM INDEPENDENT 1988-1989.
Indexed 1856-1862, 1930-1941, 1943-1964, 1966, 1968, 1970-1987.

WEST LONDON TIMES 1860-1867.

KENSINGTON AND HAMMERSMITH REPORTER 1879-1891; continued as WEST LONDON REPORTER 1892-1906.

FULHAM CHRONICLE 1888-1999; continued as FULHAM AND HAMMERSMITH CHRONICLE 2000 to date.
Indexed 1927-1991.

WEST LONDON ADVERTISER 1892-1896; continued as WEST LONDON ADVERTISER AND WEST LONDON NEWS 1896-1905.

WEST END PRESS 1900-1904 (gaps); continued as WEST END WEEKLY EXPRESS 1905-1906; continued as HAMMERSMITH AND SHEPHERDS BUSH WEEKLY EXPRESS 1906; continued as HAMMERSMITH, SHEPHERDS BUSH AND KENSINGTON WEEKLY EXPRESS 1906; continued as HAMMERSMITH, SHEPHERDS BUSH AND KENSINGTON WEEKLY EXPRESS AND WEST END PRESS 1906-1907.

WEST LONDON AND FULHAM TIMES 1904-1915.

FULHAM GAZETTE 1919-1927; continued as FULHAM AND WEST LONDON GAZETTE 1927-1928; continued as WEST LONDON AND FULHAM GAZETTE 1928-1971.
Indexed 1927-1960, 1962-1964, 1968 and 1970-1971.

WEST LONDON POST, SHEPHERDS BUSH, ACTON, HAMMERSMITH 1939; continued as ACTON GAZETTE AND WEST LONDON POST 1939-1951; continued as SHEPHERDS BUSH GAZETTE AND WEST LONDON POST 1955-1958; continued as HAMMERSMITH POST [local edition of above] 1955-1959; continued as SHEPHERDS BUSH GAZETTE, HAMMERSMITH POST 1960-1983; continued as SHEPHERDS BUSH-HAMMERSMITH GAZETTE 1984-1988; continued as THE GAZETTE 1988-1989; continued as HAMMERSMITH AND SHEPHERDS BUSH GAZETTE 1989; continued as HAMMERSMITH, FULHAM AND SHEPHERDS BUSH GAZETTE 1989 to 1998; continued as HAMMERSMITH AND SHEPHERDS BUSH GAZETTE 1999 to date.
Indexed 1970-1991.

FULHAM AND HAMMERSMITH ADVERTISER 1949-1957; continued as FULHAM AND HAMMERSMITH NEWS 1957-1958.

WEST LONDON ADVERTISER 1981-1987.

HAMMERSMITH NEWS AND FULHAM POST 1983-1987; continued as HAMMERSMITH NEWS AND POST 1987.

HAMMERSMITH AND FULHAM GUARDIAN 1984-1986; continued as FULHAM AND HAMMERSMITH GUARDIAN 1986-1988; continued as HAMMERSMITH AND FULHAM GUARDIAN 1988-1991; continued as HAMMERSMITH, FULHAM AND CHISWICK GUARDIAN 1991-2001.

WEST LONDON RECORDER 1985-1988; continued as CHISWICK, FULHAM AND HAMMERSMITH RECORDER 1988-1990.

FULHAM POST 1987-1991.
Merged with Hammersmith Post to form the Hammersmith and Fulham Post.

FULHAM TIMES 1987-1989; continued as HAMMERSMITH AND FULHAM TIMES 1989 to date.
The Hammersmith and Fulham Independent merged with the above in 1989.

HAMMERSMITH POST 1989-1991.
Merged with Fulham Post to form Hammersmith and Fulham Post.

HAMMERSMITH AND FULHAM POST 1992-1998.

4. CUTTINGS COLLECTIONS

Collections of cuttings and printed ephemera including files on Wormwood Scrubs Prison, Chelsea, Queens Park Rangers and Fulham Football Clubs, Hammersmith Broadway and its development and Fulham Palace.

For details of special collections relating to the White City Exhibitions and William Morris see p.143, and Sir William Bull see p.170.

5. DIRECTORIES

5.2 London, county and general directories

LONDON
Pigot and Co.
1826/27, 1839 (reprint).

LONDON
Post Office (Various publishers until 1836; from 1837 Kelly's).
1846 (reprint), 1859 (part), 1860, 1872, 1880, 1881 (part), 1915, 1917, 1919, 1921, 1923-1930, 1935-1991 (some vols incomplete).

LONDON
Allen and Morton.
1867 (part).

LONDON
Green's South-West London Directory.
1869.

LONDON
Post Office Suburban (Kelly's).
1876 (part).

MIDDLESEX
Pigot and Co.
1839.

5.3 Local directories

ACTON
Kelly's.
1940.

CHELSEA
The Court Guide and Commercial Directory (Green and Co.).
1873/74.
Covers other areas including Shepherds Bush.

CHISWICK
Kelly's.
1939.

HAMMERSMITH AND KENSINGTON
R.G. Rist.
1865.

HAMMMERSMITH
Cordingley's Court Guide and Directory.
1875, 1876 (includes Fulham).

HAMMERSMITH AND SHEPHERD'S BUSH
Kelly's.
1899/1900-1939/40 (gaps).

KENSINGTON AND HAMMERSMITH
Simpsons.
1863.

KENSINGTON
Kelly's.
1950.

KILBURN
Kelly's.
1937, 1940.
Includes College Park.

WEST KENSINGTON AND HAMMERSMITH
Hutchings and Crowsley; later Kelly's.
1885/86, 1889/90-1898/99.
Includes Fulham.

WEST KENSINGTON, WALHAM GREEN AND FULHAM
Kelly's.
1899/1900-1921/22

WEST KENSINGTON, FULHAM AND WALHAM GREEN
Kelly's.
1922/23-1939/40.

6. ELECTORAL REGISTERS

MIDDLESEX
1802, 1837/38, 1843/44-1846/47.

CHELSEA [including FULHAM AND HAMMERSMITH]
1881-1885.

FULHAM
1885/86-1964 (gaps).

HAMMERSMITH
1886-1964 (gaps).

LONDON BOROUGH OF HAMMERSMITH; later LONDON BOROUGH OF
HAMMERSMITH AND FULHAM
1965 to date.

7. ILLUSTRATIONS

About 600 paintings and other illustrations of Fulham and Hammersmith. The majority are of local
scenes but there are also some works by local artists.

About 60,000 photographs of Hammersmith and Fulham, dating from the 1870s to present day.
Mainly 1900-1910 and 1970 to date.

A complete photographic survey of the borough was undertaken in the 1970s. Photography of new
development continues. Collection of colour photographs of the borough's streets, buildings and
houses taken by Hammersmith and Fulham Historic Buildings Group in 1995/96.

About 3,000 colour transparencies and 800 glass lantern slides. Copy negatives and prints made from
many of these.

Special collections:

CECIL FRENCH BEQUEST
53 pictures, including 25 works by Sir Edward Coley Burne-Jones and works by Lord Leighton, Sir
Lawrence Alma-Tadema, F. G. Watts, W. J. Waterhouse, Albert Moore and others. The Bequest is on
long-term loan to Leighton House Art Gallery and Museum.

SAMUEL MARTIN BEQUEST
Paintings, mainly local views, presented by Samuel Martin, Librarian of Hammersmith 1889-1919.
Includes a number of paintings by Evacustes Phipson.

For details of special collection relating to the White City Exhibitions see p.143.

8. MAPS

8.1 General maps

Local maps including those of John Rocque 1741-1745, Salter's map of Hammersmith 1830, Roberts'
map of Hammersmith 1853, and Maclure's map of Fulham 1853. Local authority maps. Goad
shopping plans of Hammersmith Broadway/King Street, Shepherds Bush Green and Fulham
Broadway/North End Road 1983 to date.

8.2 Ordnance Survey maps

6 INCHES: 1 MILE (1: 10,560)
1874, 1920, 1938, 1948-1950, 1958.

25 INCHES: 1 MILE; 1: 2,500 (approx. 25 inches: 1 mile)
1869-1874, 1894-1896, 1915-1916, 1935 (part), 1951-1953.

60 INCHES: 1 MILE (1: 1,056)
1869-1874, 1894-1896, 1906-1921. Revision sheets 1935-1939, 1946, 1949 (incomplete).

1: 1,250 (approx. 50 inches: 1 mile)
1951-1953, 1971, 1996. Revision sheets 1960s-1992.

9. AUDIO-VISUAL ITEMS

Small collection of gramophone and tape recordings, mostly music by local composers or recordings by local orchestras, bands and schools.

Small collection of reel to reel films and videotapes of local events. No viewing equipment available.

Oral history tapes produced by Hammersmith and Fulham Ethnic Communities Oral History Project, North Kensington Local History Project and White City Community History Project.

10. COLLECTIONS OF MUSEUM OBJECTS

Items reflecting social history of the borough: commemorative material, examples of local manufacture, prizes awarded by schools and clubs, memorabilia, publicity material.

Special collections:

POTTERY COLLECTION
Items made at the Fulham Pottery from the 17th to 20th centuries; Martinware (some made at Fulham Pottery, but most made at Southall); tiles and a lustre vase by William de Morgan, Sands End Pottery.

11. LOCAL AUTHORITY RECORDS AND RECORDS OF PREDECESSOR AUTHORITIES

11.1 Fulham Metropolitan Borough area

FULHAM PARISH

The Vestry was reconstituted with additional powers in 1886 after Fulham District Board of Works was abolished.

Vestry minutes 1646-1693, 1721-1765, 1776-1900.

Churchwardens' and Overseers' minutes 1868-1875.

Committee minutes:

  Assessment Committee 1899-1900.

  Baths and Washhouses Committee 1899-1901.

  Cartage Committee 1885-1900.

  Cemetery Committee 1896-1901.

  Finance Committee 1885-1900.

  Law and Parliamentary Committee 1885-1900.

  Library Committee 1899-1902.

  Lighting Committee 1890-1897.

  Lighting, Electric Lighting and Dust Destructor Committee 1898-1901.

  New Streets Committee 1889-1900.

  Sanitary Committee 1885-1901.

  Special Committees 1866-1877, 1886-1901.

  Vestry Committee [later Town Hall Committee] 1887-1901.

  Works and General Purposes Committee 1885-1900.

Abstract of accounts 1887-1897.

Churchwardens' accounts 1637-1674, 1711-1791.

Burial records:

  Fulham Burial Ground, Fulham Palace Road, registers of burials and notices of interment 1896-1900. *Indexed 1896-1899.*

Highway and paving records:

  Highways Board minutes 1836-1856.

  Surveyors' accounts 1664, 1770-1808, 1827-1836.

  Highways Board cash book 1836-1856.

  Highways Board labour book 1843-1856.

Poor Law records:

  Workhouse Committee minutes 1771-1820.

  Select Vestry for the Poor minutes 1820-1823, 1826-1833.

  Overseers' accounts 1625-1642, 1712-1838.

  Apprenticeship indentures 1666-1750.

  Settlement examinations 1778-1808, 1817-1827.

  Workhouse provisions accounts 1818-1824.

  List of workhouse inmates 1785/86.

Public health records:

  Drainage applications and plans 1886-1900. *Address index.*

Register of infectious diseases 1890-1893.
Returns of infant deaths 1876-1891.
Surveyor's records:
Case files and plans 1886-1900.
Returns of street renumbering 1881-1891.
Rate assessments and valuation lists 1625-1675 (gaps), 1712-1900 (some assessments appear in Vestry minutes, Churchwardens' accounts, Overseers' accounts and Highway Surveyors' accounts). *Street index 1838-1886.*
Terrier of lands and inventory of funds belonging to the parish 1839.

FULHAM BURIAL BOARD
Taken over by Fulham Vestry in 1896.
Minutes 1863-1896.
Fulham Burial Ground, Fulham Palace Road, registers of burials and notices of interment 1865-1896.
Indexed 1865-1896.

FULHAM COMMISSIONERS FOR PUBLIC LIBRARIES AND MUSEUMS
Taken over by Fulham Vestry in 1899.
Fulham Public Library accessions book 1887-1890.

FULHAM DISTRICT BOARD OF WORKS
Board covering the parishes of Fulham and Hammersmith.
Minutes 1855-1886.
Committee minutes:
Bye-laws and Parliamentary Committee 1859-1862.
Cartage Committee 1875-1886.
Finance Committee 1856-1886.
Fulham General Purposes Committee [also known as the Fulham Committee] 1866-1871.
Fulham Sanitary Committee 1866-1868.
General Purposes Committee 1858-1866, 1869-1870.
Hammersmith General Purposes Committee [also known as District Committee and the Hammersmith Committee] 1866-1871.
General and Sanitary Committee 1874-1886.
Hammersmith Sanitary Committee 1866-1868.
Law and Parliamentary Committee 1874-1886.
Lighting and General Purposes Committee 1856-1858.
Parliamentary Committee 1862-1864.
Sanitary Committee 1861-1866.
Sanitary and Nuisance Removal Committee 1856-1859.
Sanitary and Sewers Committee 1859-1860.
Sanitary, Sewers, Main Drainage and Embankment Committee 1860-1861.
Sewers Committee 1856-1859.
Special and Emergency Committees 1856-1887.
Works Committee 1874-1886.
Medical Officer of Health annual reports 1857-1886.

Public health records:

Drainage applications and plans 1860-1886. Address index.

Surveyor's Department records:

New streets records 1860-1886.

Paving apportionments 1864-1885.

Case files 1859-1886.

Railways and tramways deposited plans 1861-1885.

FULHAM METROPOLITAN BOROUGH

Council minutes 1900-1965.

Committee minutes:

Accident Prevention Committee 1946-1965.

Air Raid Precautions Committee 1936-1939.

Assessment Committee 1900-1945.

Cartage Committee 1900-1945.

Children's Safety Committee 1936-1946.

Civil Defence Committee 1941-1945, 1949-1961.

Civil Defence Emergency Committee 1939-1940.

Civil Recreation Committee 1951-1965.

Committees of Council and Special Committees 1919-1928.

Distress Committee 1905-1915.

Electricity and Lighting Committee 1907-1949.

Establishment Committee 1901-1965.

Expenditure Special Committee 1923, 1931-1934.

Finance Committee 1900-1965.

General Emergency Committee 1939.

Grading and Advisory Committee 1924-1934.

Housing Committee 1920, 1924-1965.

Joint Advisory Committee of Metropolitan Boroughs of Fulham and Hammersmith 1963-1964.

Joint Works Committee 1949-1965.

Law and Parliamentary Committee 1902-1965.

Maternity and Child Welfare Committee and others 1918-1948.

Planning Committee 1962-1964.

Post-War Committee and Sub-committee 1943-1944.

Public Health Committee 1902-1964.

Public Libraries Committee 1903-1965.

Public Shelters Committee 1940-1943.

Staff Committee 1935-1965.

Wages Advisory Committee 1920-1923.

War Damage Committee 1944-1947.

War Emergency Committee 1940-1941.

Welfare Committee 1963-1964.

Works Committee 1900-1907.

Works and Highways Committee 1907-1965.

Burial records:
    Fulham Burial Ground, Fulham Palace Road:
        Registers of burials 1900-1909.
        Notices of interments 1900-1960.
    Fulham New Cemetery, North Sheen:
        Notices of interments 1909-1964.
        Applications for purchase of graves 1909-1964.
Civil Defence records:
    Air Raid incidents register 1940-1945.
Clerk's Department:
    Lillie Ward Committee for the Prevention and Relief of Distress minutes and accounts
    1914-1915.
Engineer and Surveyor's Department records:
    War damaged property files and index 1940s.
Public health records:
    Baby clinic cards 1930s-1940s.
    Drainage applications and plans 1900-1965. *Address index.*
Public libraries records 1900-1965.
Shipping records:
    S.S. Fulham ledgers 1938-1947 [colliers supplying Fulham Power Station].
Treasurer's Department records 1900-1965.
Ratebooks and valuation lists 1900-1964.

11.2 Hammersmith Metropolitan Borough area

HAMMERSMITH PARISH
The vestry was reconstituted with additional powers in 1886 following the abolition of the Fulham District Board of Works.
Vestry minutes 1730-1900.
Committee minutes:
    Assessments Committee 1899-1900.
    Cartage Committee 1886-1900.
    Cemetery Committee 1896-1900.
    Electric Lighting Committee 1896-1900.
    Finance Committee 1886-1900.
    General and Sanitary Committee [later Public Health Committee] 1886-1900.
    Law and Parliamentary Committee 1886-1900.
    Letting Committee 1892-1898.
    Public Library Committee 1896-1900.
    Special Committees 1886-1900.
    Town Hall Committee 1898-1900.
    Works Committee 1886-1900.
    Other Committees 1828-1891.
Medical Officer of Health reports 1887-1900.
Churchwardens' accounts 1656-1715, 1773-1892.

Burial records:

    Hammersmith Burial Ground, Margravine Road, registers of burials 1896-1900.

Highway and lighting records:

    Highways Board minutes 1836-1855.

    Highways Surveyors' accounts 1822-1856.

    Lighting Inspectors' minutes 1843-1856.

Poor Law records:

    Select Vestry for the Poor minutes 1823-1837.

    Overseers' minutes 1848-1900.

    Overseers' accounts 1795-1800, 1822-1830, 1856-1889.

    Apprenticeship indentures 1810-1832.

    Removal orders 1798-1833.

    Workhouse inmates register 1730-1768.

Public health records:

    Drainage applications and plans 1886-1900. *Address index.*

    Returns of infant deaths 1871-1894.

Surveyor's records:

    New streets letter books 1886-1900.

    Plans 1886-1900.

    Railways and tramways deposited plans 1886-1900.

Rate assessments and valuation lists 1773-1900. *Street index 1838-1906.*

Census returns: heads of households 1821, 1831.

HAMMERSMITH BURIAL BOARD

Taken over by Hammersmith Vestry in 1896.

Minutes 1863-1896.

Hammersmith Burial Ground, Margravine Road, registers of burials 1869-1900.

HAMMERSMITH PUBLIC LIBRARIES AND MUSEUMS COMMISSIONERS

Taken over by Hammersmith Vestry in 1896.

Minutes 1888-1896.

Letter books 1888-1900.

HAMMERSMITH METROPOLITAN BOROUGH

Council minutes 1900-1965.

Committee minutes:

    Accounts Committee 1922-1929.

    Air Raid Precautions Committee 1937-1939.

    Allotments Committee 1920-1946.

    Assessments Committee 1900-1920.

    Baths and Washhouses Committee [later Baths Committee] 1903-1945, 1953-1965.

    Cartage Cemetery and Town Hall Committee 1902-1921.

    Civil Defence Committee 1940-1945.

    Community Centre Committee [later Community Recreation Committee] 1938-1945.

    Council and Electricity Department Joint Works Committee 1938-1947.

    Council Employees Joint Committee 1937-1955.

Council Staff Joint Committee 1922-1948.

Distress Committee 1906-1915.

Electricity Committee 1913-1945.

Electricity and Lighting Committee 1900-1912.

Emergency Committee 1939-1940.

Establishment Committee 1922-1929.

Executive Committee 1939, 1941-1943.

Executive and Civil Defence Committee 1940-1941.

Finance Committee 1900-1945.

Finance and General Purposes Committee 1915-1929.

General Purposes Committee 1900-1902, 1930-1945.

Hammersmith Children's Safety Committee 1936-1943.

Hammersmith Old People's Welfare Association Executive Committee 1950-1963.

Hammersmith Savings Committee 1962-1964.

Housing Improvements and Developments Committee [later Housing and Town Planning Committee] 1918-1945.

Law and Parliamentary Committee 1900-1929.

Libraries Committee [later Public Libraries Committee] 1900-1945.

Maternity and Child Welfare Committee 1918-1945.

Public Health Committee 1900-1965.

Rating and Valuation Committee 1901-1916.

Salaries and Wages Committee 1917-1921.

Special Committees 1900-1947.

Special Emergency Committee 1938.

Special Purposes Committee 1902-1921.

Town Hall Committee 1936-1945.

Works Committee 1900-1921.

Works, Cartage and Cemetery Committee 1921-1929.

Works, Parks and Cemetery Committee 1921-1945.

Burial records:

Hammersmith Burial Ground, Margravine Road, registers of burials 1900-1952.

Hammersmith New Cemetery, Mortlake, registers of burials 1926-1953. Indexes 1948-1953.

Civil Defence records:

Air Raid Incidents register 1940-1945.

Files 1935-1945.

Clerk's Department records:

Committee papers and files c.1900-1965.

Golden Book of Hammersmith 1907-1965.

Contracts 1924-1940.

Letter books and other records c.1900-1965.

Engineer and Surveyor's Department records:

Case files and plans c.1900-1940s.

Drainage applications and plans 1900-1965. *Address index.*

Public health records:

Compulsory purchase order files 1936-1951.

Hammersmith Old People's Welfare Association records 1950-1956.
Slum clearance files 1930-1952.
Ratebooks and valuation lists 1900-1964. *Street index 1900-1906.*

11.3 London Borough of Hammersmith and Fulham

Council minutes 1964 to date.
Committee minutes 1964 to date. *Closed until 30 years old.*
Amalgamation of Metropolitan Boroughs of Fulham and Hammersmith records 1963-1965.
Environmental Health Department:
     Drainage applications and plans 1964-1986. *Address index.*

12. LOCAL RECORDS OF CENTRAL GOVERNMENT

INLAND REVENUE:
Duties on land values [Domesday Survey] 1911. Volumes covering Metropolitan Boroughs of Fulham and Hammersmith.

13. RECORDS OF OTHER PUBLIC AUTHORITIES

FULHAM BOARD OF GUARDIANS
Records of vaccination 1868-1948.

16. RECORDS OF PARISHES

ALL SAINTS FULHAM
Vestry minute book 1877-1891.
Churchwardens' rates and accounts 1826-1886.

CHRIST CHURCH FULHAM
Accounts 1977-1987.

ST ANDREW FULHAM FIELDS
Plan of seating layout 1884.

ST BARNABAS KENSINGTON
Unity experiment with Munster Park Methodist Church, Fulham.
Baptism registers 1969-1975.

ST DIONIS PARSONS GREEN [Fulham]
Church rolls 1920-1930.
Pew rents 1905-1931.
Clothing and club accounts 1903-1932.

ST JOHN THE EVANGELIST HAMMERSMITH
Communicants rolls 1860-1931.
Service registers 1927-1954.
Minutes, deeds, accounts, plans, correspondence 1843-1955.

ST PAUL HAMMERSMITH
Registers and curates' note books:
> Baptism 1664-1960.
> Marriage 1664/65-1972.
> Burial 1664/65-1857.

Banns books 1838-1981 (gaps).
Service registers 1868-1990 (gaps).
Vestry minutes 1926-1976.
Parochial Church Council minutes 1920-1984.
Churchwardens' accounts 1656-1972 (gaps).
Paper relating to benefice and church fabric 1629-1983.

17. RECORDS OF NON-ANGLICAN PLACES OF WORSHIP

17.1 Non-conformist churches

ALBION CONGREGATIONAL CHURCH, *Dalling Road, Hammersmith*
Membership list 1926.
Scrapbook of cuttings, correspondence and photographs 1938-1940.

ASKEW ROAD METHODIST CHURCH [formerly BASSEIN PARK WESLEYAN CHAPEL (1866-1890); SIR WILLIAM MCARTHUR MEMORIAL CHAPEL (1890-1897)], *Askew Road, Hammersmith*
Minutes 1869-1987.
Accounts 1866-1987.
Roll of members 1890-1905, 1957-1964.

BARCLAY METHODIST MISSION HALL, *Effie Road, Fulham*
Baptism registers 1934-1948.

BETHEL METHODIST CHURCH, *North End Road, Fulham*
Minutes 1895-1969.
Correspondence and papers 1870-c.1889.

BROADWAY CONGREGATIONAL CHURCH [formerly WHITE HORSE YARD MEETING HOUSE; GEORGE YARD CHAPEL], *Brook Green Road [renamed Shepherds Bush Road], Hammersmith*
Baptism registers 1900-1969.
Minutes 1792-1971.

Accounts 1724-1964.
Deeds and papers 1720-1916.

DALLING ROAD METHODIST CHURCH, *Dalling Road, Hammersmith*
Closed in 1955.
Minutes 1869-1911, 1933-1976.
Accounts 1869-1975.

EBENEZER METHODIST CHAPEL, *North End Road, Fulham*
Minutes 1952-1968.
Accounts 1936-1969.

FULHAM BAPTIST CHURCH, *Dawes Road, Fulham*
Missionary Council Minutes 1935-1959.

FULHAM PALACE ROAD CONGREGATIONAL CHURCH, *Fulham Palace Road, Fulham*
Registers:
>   Baptism 1906-1924.
>   Marriage 1909-1919.
Minutes 1925-1963.
Sunday School records 1907-1933.

HAMMERSMITH METHODIST CIRCUIT
Acton, Battersea, Bayswater, Bloomsbury, Old Brentford, Brentford, Chelsea, Ealing, Feltham, Fulham, Hammersmith, New Hampton, Hanwell, Heston (Lampton), Hounslow and Isleworth, Kensington, Wandsworth.
Baptism registers 1849-1937.
Minutes, accounts and other records 1811-1969.

ISLEWORTH WESLEYAN METHODIST CHAPEL, *North Street, Isleworth, Middlesex*
Papers 1816-1854.

KENSAL ROAD METHODIST CHURCH, *Kensal Road, Kensington*
Minutes 1926-1840.

KINGSTON WESLEYAN METHODIST CHAPEL, *Brick Lane, Kingston, Surrey*
Correspondence and papers 1833-1835.

LANCASTER ROAD METHODIST CHAPEL, *Lancaster Road, Kensington*
Minutes and papers 1877-1953.

MUNSTER PARK METHODIST CHURCH, *Fulham Road, Fulham*
Registers:
>   Baptism 1880-1949.
>   Marriage 1883-1995.

Minutes 1880-1953, 1984-1994.
Accounts 1895-1961.

MUNSTER ROAD METHODIST CHURCH, *Munster Road, Fulham*
Baptism registers 1920-1949.
Minutes 1908-1914, 1928-1953.

OAKLANDS CONGREGATIONAL CHURCH, *Uxbridge Road, Hammersmith*
Registers:
      Baptism 1886-1932.
      Marriage 1887-1889.
Minutes 1856-1972.
Accounts 1927-1958.
Roll of members 1891-1970.
Plan 1890.

OLD OAK METHODIST CHURCH, *The Fairway, East Acton, Acton, Middlesex*
Minutes 1952-1970.
Accounts 1938-1959.
Correspondence and papers 1926-1963.

RIVERCOURT METHODIST CHURCH [formerly WATERLOO STREET WESLEYAN CHAPEL (1809-1874)], *King Street, Hammersmith*
Minutes 1843-1918.
Accounts 1811-1896.

ROYAL HILL METHODIST CHAPEL, *Queens Road, Bayswater, Westminster*
Baptism registers 1843-1908.

SHEPHERDS BUSH BAPTIST TABERNACLE, *Shepherds Bush Road, Hammersmith*
Correspondence 1890-1919.

SHEPHERDS BUSH ROAD METHODIST CHURCH [formerly WEST KENSINGTON PARK WESLEYAN METHODIST CHURCH], *Shepherds Bush Road, Hammersmith*
Marriage registers 1881-1915.
Minutes 1879-1968.
Accounts 1926-1973.

TWICKENHAM WESLEYAN METHODIST CHAPEL, *Holly Road, Twickenham, Middlesex*
Papers 1837-1862

WALHAM GREEN METHODIST CHURCH, *Fulham Road, Fulham*
Registers:
      Baptism 1926-1965.
      Marriage 1899-1903.

Minutes 1881-1974.
Correspondence 1891-1970.

WALHAM GROVE METHODIST CHURCH, *Walham Grove, Fulham*
Baptism registers 1866-1962.
Minutes 1893-1971.

WEST KENSINGTON CONGREGATIONAL CHURCH [later WEST KENSINGTON UNITED REFORMED CHURCH], *Castletown Road, Fulham*
Registers:
      Baptism 1885-1977.
      Marriage 1885-1973.
Minutes 1885-1977.
Roll of members 1885-1974.

17.2 Synagogues

HAMMERSMITH AND WEST KENSINGTON SYNAGOGUE, *Brook Green, Hammersmith*
Minutes, accounts, membership lists, correspondence, magazines 1890-1990s.

18. RECORDS OF RELIGIOUS ORGANISATIONS

BENEDICTINE CONVENT, *Hammersmith Road, Hammersmith*
Deeds 1799-1866.

CONVENT OF THE INSTITUTE OF THE BLESSED VIRGIN MARY, *Hammersmith Road, Hammersmith*
Deeds and other records 1672-1792.

CONVENT DE NOTRE DAME DE BONS SECOURS DE TROYES IN LONDON, *Upper Park Road, Haverstock Hill, Hampstead*
Accounts 1872-1905.

20. RECORDS OF ALMSHOUSES

ELIZABETHAN ALMSHOUSE CHARITY, *Wickham House, Putney Hill, Wandsworth*
Minutes 1963-1981

FULHAM WASTE LAND AND LYGON ALMSHOUSES, *Fulham Palace Road, Fulham*
Minutes 1907-1973.
Accounts 1897-1971.
Deeds and correspondence 1825-1939.

HAMMERSMITH WASTE LAND ALMSHOUSES, *Becklow Road, Hammersmith*
Minutes 1810-1849.

SIR WILLIAM POWELL ALMSHOUSES, *Burlington Road; Church Gate, Fulham*
Minutes 1865-1935.
Deeds 1729-1974.
Accounts and papers 1872-1967.

21. RECORDS OF HOSPITALS, ASYLUMS AND DISPENSARIES

FULHAM INFIRMARY/HOSPITAL, *Fulham Palace Road, Fulham*
Plans 1876-1878, 1911.
Visitors' reports 1912-1919.

WEST LONDON HOSPITAL, *Hammersmith Road, Hammersmith*
Administrative records 1856-1993. *Closed until 30 years old.*
Medical records 1899-1979. *Closed until 100 years old.*

WESTERN HOSPITAL, *Seagrave Road, Fulham*
Medical records 1885-1886.
Report books 1922-1936.
Minutes 1953-1968.
Staff registers 1877-1951.

23. RECORDS OF SCHOOLS AND COLLEGES

AVONMORE SCHOOL, *Avonmore Road, West Kensington, Fulham*
Admission registers 1940-1970.

BURLINGTON SCHOOL [later BURLINGTON DANES SCHOOL (1975-)], *Boyle Street, Westminster (-1936); Wood Lane, Hammersmith (1936-)*
Minutes 1700-1992.
Accounts 1776-1977 (gaps).
Admission registers 1826-1943 (gaps).
Staff registers 1882-1937.
Correspondence, inventories, visitors' books, photographs, magazines 1767-1995.

ELLERSLIE ROAD SCHOOL, *Ellerslie Road, Shepherds Bush, Hammersmith*
Admission registers 1894-1991.
Log books 1932-1939, 1946-1969.

FULHAM CENTRAL SCHOOL [later BISHOPS PARK SECONDARY SCHOOL (1951-)], *Finlay Street, Fulham*
Admission registers 1929-1961.

GODOLPHIN SCHOOL, Great Church Lane, Hammersmith (-1862); *Iffley Road, Hammersmith* **(1862-)**
Minutes 1855-1873, 1893-1904.
Rule book 1895.

GODOLPHIN AND LATYMER SCHOOL, *Iffley Road, Hammersmith*
Minutes 1903-1918.
Admission and attendance registers 1905-1976.
Correspondence, magazines, programmes, photographs, 1905-1990.

HARWOOD ROAD SCHOOL, *Harwood Road, Fulham*
Admission registers 1873-1939, 1958-1991.
Log books 1873-1991.
Minutes 1873-1883.

LILLIE ROAD SCHOOL, *Lillie Road, Fulham*
Infants log book 1891-1912.

MUNSTER ROAD SCHOOL, *Filmer Road, Fulham*
Plans 1890-1897, 1937.
Schoolkeepers' diary 1923-1929.

QUEENS MANOR SCHOOL, *Lysia Street, Fulham*
Admission registers 1953-1977.
Log books 1960-1991.

ST HELEN'S ROMAN CATHOLIC INFANTS' AND GIRLS' SCHOOL [later SACRED HEART JUNIOR SCHOOL (1894-)], *Brook Green, Hammersmith (-1894); Hammersmith Road, Hammersmith (1894-)*
Log books and cash book 1872-1913.

ST JOHN'S NATIONAL SCHOOLS [later ST JOHN'S CHURCH OF ENGLAND SCHOOL], *Bradmore Lane, Hammersmith (-1871); Glenthorne Road, Hammersmith (1871-1944); Macbeth Street, Hammersmith (1944-)*
Admission registers 1933-1971.
Log books 1863-1983.

ST PAUL'S NATIONAL SCHOOLS [later ST PAUL'S CHURCH OF ENGLAND SCHOOL], *Queen Caroline Street, Hammersmith*
Minutes 1859-1920.
Accounts 1845-1927.
Log books 1863-1925.

SHERBROOKE ROAD SCHOOL, *Sherbrooke Road, Fulham*
Girls log books 1885-1897, 1908-1913.

STAR LANE SCHOOL [later STAR ROAD SCHOOL], *Star Road, West Kensington, Fulham*
Log books 1876-1897 (Boys), 1880-1906 (Girls), 1899-1913 (Infants).

THE VICTORIA SCHOOL, *Becklow Road, Hammersmith*
Schoolkeepers' diaries 1930-1949, 1955-1965.

28. RECORDS OF MILITARY AND ARMED BODIES

HAMMERSMITH ARMED OR VOLUNTEER ASSOCIATION
Printed notice 1798.
Committee minutes 1803.

HOME GUARD
Log book, Battalion Orderly Officer, Fulham 1944.
Photograph album, Hammersmith Civil Defence Warders' Service 1945.

29. RECORDS OF ASSOCIATIONS, CLUBS AND SOCIETIES

6TH FULHAM GIRL GUIDES, *Church Hall, Chesilton Road, Fulham*
Log book 1924-1966.

7TH FULHAM (CHRIST CHURCH) BOY SCOUTS, *Studdridge Street, Fulham*
Minutes, correspondence and papers 1910-1969.

ANTI-COMMON MARKET LEAGUE AND FEDERATION OF ANTI-COMMON MARKET GROUPS, *52 Fulham High Street, Fulham*
Correspondence and papers 1972-1985.

BARONS COURT CONSTITUENCY LABOUR PARTY, *Hammersmith Town Hall, King Street, Hammersmith*
Minutes, accounts and papers 1950-1970.

BISHOP CREIGHTON HOUSE, *378 Lillie Road, Fulham*
Minutes, reports, correspondence and papers c.1908-1970.

BROADWAY CHURCH MEN'S SICK BENEFIT SOCIETY (1905-1938); [later BROADWAY CONGREGATIONAL FRIENDLY SOCIETY (1938-)], *Brook Green Road [renamed Shepherds Bush Road], Hammersmith*
Minutes, reports, accounts 1905-1970.

CHELSEA CONSERVATIVE AND CONSTITUTIONAL UNION: HAMMERSMITH BRANCH, *Ravenscourt Villa, Ravenscourt Square, Hammersmith*
Minutes 1869-1873.

COMMUNITY FORUM FOR HAMMERSMITH AND FULHAM, *210 Munster Road, Fulham*
Minutes 1974-1987.

FULHAM BOWLING CLUB, *Bishops Park, Fulham*
Minutes and membership register 1909-1952.

FULHAM DRAMA ASSOCIATION
Minutes 1953-1956.

FULHAM FIELD CLUB AND LITERARY AND SCIENTIFIC SOCIETY, *635 Fulham Road, Fulham*
Minutes and accounts, 1904-1905.

FULHAM GRAMOPHONE SOCIETY, *Central Library, 598 Fulham Road, Fulham*
Minutes and correspondence 1945-1958.

FULHAM GROUP OF THE CAMPAIGN FOR NUCLEAR DISARMAMENT, *23 Colehill Lane, Fulham*
Correspondence, circulars and papers 1960-1966.

FULHAM HOUSING IMPROVEMENT SOCIETY, 378 Lillie Road, Fulham (1927-1930); *91 Dawes Road, Fulham (1930-1968)*
Minutes, reports, accounts and papers, 1927-1968.

FULHAM JUBILEE CELEBRATION COMMITTEE, *Mission Hall, Parsons Green, Fulham*
Minutes 1887.

FULHAM PALACE MEADOW ALLOTMENTS ASSOCIATION, *Bishops Park, Fulham*
Minutes 1948-1983.

FULHAM PHILANTHROPIC SOCIETY
Minutes 1935-1976.

FULHAM PRIMITIVE METHODIST SLATE CLUB (-1906) [later FULHAM PRIMITIVE METHODIST SICK AND PROVIDENT SOCIETY (1906-)], *Wandsworth Bridge Road, Fulham*
Membership forms 1893-1940.

FULHAM RATEPAYERS' ASSOCIATION (1935-1964) [later FULHAM AND HAMMERSMITH RATEPAYERS' ASSOCIATION (1964-1986)]
Minutes, accounts, papers 1935-1986.

FULHAM SOCIETY, *8 Edenhurst Avenue, Fulham*
Minutes and newsletters 1971-1977.

FULHAM AND SOUTH KENSINGTON YOUNG MEN'S CHRISTIAN ASSOCIATION,
641-643 Fulham Road, Fulham
Minutes 1976-1989.
Reports, correspondence and papers 1946-2000.

FULHAM UNITED CHARITIES
Minutes, accounts, correspondence 1786-2000.
Some records closed until 100 years old.

GREEK CYPRIOT ASSOCIATION OF FULHAM AND HAMMERSMITH, *2 Royal Parade,*
Dawes Road, Fulham
Minutes and correspondence 1971-1990.

HAMMERSMITH ALLOTMENT AND GARDENS ASSOCIATION
Minutes, accounts, programmes, photographs 1963-1987.

HAMMERSMITH FILM SOCIETY, *Hammersmith Town Hall, King Street, Hammersmith*
Accounts 1949-1959.

HAMMERSMITH AND FULHAM HISTORIC BUILDINGS GROUP
Correspondence files 1987-1998.
Photographic survey of borough 1995.

HAMMERSMITH AND FULHAM TRADES COUNCIL, *190 Shepherds Bush Road,*
Hammersmith
Minutes 1988-1996.

HAMMERSMITH LITERARY AND SCIENTIFIC SOCIETY, *Vestry Hall, Broadway,*
Hammersmith
Minutes, membership lists, programmes 1877-1896.

HAMMERSMITH SOCIETY
Minutes, correspondence and subject files 1962-c.1988.

HAMPSHIRE HOUSE TRUST, *Hampshire Hog Lane, Hammersmith*
Minutes, reports and correspondence 1905-1952.
'Parliament' correspondence 1907-1951.
Photographic Society minutes and prints 1919-1951.

LONDON CORINTHIAN SAILING CLUB, *Lower Mall, Hammersmith*
Minutes 1894-1940.
Attendance book 1896-1903.

MUNSTER PARK CYCLING CLUB, *Wesleyan Schoolroom, Chesilton Road, Fulham*
Minutes, accounts and programmes 1901-1934.

PETERBOROUGH BENEVOLENT SOCIETY, *Fulham*
Minutes 1853-1962.
Reports 1835-1938.
Accounts 1893-1968.
Other records 1833-1968.

POSTMEN'S FEDERATION: HAMMERSMITH BRANCH (-1920) [later UNION OF POST OFFICE WORKERS: HAMMERSMITH BRANCH (1920-)]
Minutes 1909-1917, 1935-1954.
Accounts 1939-1949.

SHEPHERDS BUSH PHILANTHROPIC SOCIETY, *163 Goldhawk Road, Hammersmith*
Minutes 1952-1966.
Reports 1910-1926.

SIR OSWALD STOLL FOUNDATION, *446 Fulham Road, Fulham*
Correspondence, tenants' files, accounts c.1920-1985.

SOUTH HAMMERSMITH DIVISIONAL LABOUR PARTY, *80 Dalling Road, Hammersmith*
Minutes 1939-1954.

TASSO TABERNACLE SICK AND PROVIDENT SOCIETY (1904-1939) [later TASSO TABERNACLE FRIENDLY SOCIETY (1939-1984)], *181 Greyhound Road, Fulham*
Minutes 1927-1983.
Cuttings 1948-1984.

WEST LONDON MEDICO-CHIRURGICAL SOCIETY, *West London Hospital, Hammersmith Road, Hammersmith*
Minutes, transactions and correspondence 1884-1958.

30. RECORDS OF THEATRES AND CINEMAS

KING'S THEATRE, *Hammersmith Road, Hammersmith*
Includes records of Wimbledon Theatre, Wimbledon, and Marlborough Theatre, Holloway.
Plans 1901.
Letter and cash books 1901-1940.

33. RECORDS OF BUSINESSES

A. STILES AND SONS, *37, 39 Brook Green Road [became 214 Shepherds Bush Road], Hammersmith*
Picture frame makers.
Sales books and accounts 1911-1963.

BELSHAM AND SONS, *62 Shepherds Bush Road, Hammersmith*
Printers.
Ledgers, day books, wages books 1913-1976.

BOND, W.S., *21, 22 Shepherds Bush Green, Hammersmith*
Undertakers.
Order books 1869-1976.
Account books 1872-1939.

CAMERER CUSS, *186 Uxbridge Road, Shepherds Bush, Hammersmith*
Watch and clock makers and jewellers.
Stock ledgers 1904-1975.
Account books 1923-1971.

THE COTHAM COMPANY, *92 Shaftesbury Road, Hammersmith*
Investors in cattle in Canada.
Minutes, reports, accounts, correspondence 1877-1893.

CROMWELL'S BREWERY, *King Street, Hammersmith*
Accounts 1818-1851.

FULHAM BRIDGE COMPANY
Accounts and receipts 1729-1850.
Deeds and correspondence 1768-1865.

FULHAM POTTERY, *210 New Kings Road, Fulham*
Ledgers, cash books, wages books, stock and sales books, letter books, correspondence, price lists 1865-1969.

G.W. DRAY AND SON, *Drayton Paper Works, Sulivan Road, Fulham*
Paper makers.
Ledgers, cash books, journals, personnel records 19th-20th centuries.

HAMMERSMITH BRIDGE COMPANY
Minutes, accounts, contracts, plans and papers 1824-1880.

JOHN BURGESS AND SON, *1-3 Hythe Road, Willesden Junction, Hammersmith*
Food manufacturers.
Minutes, accounts and records 1887-1953.

MANBRÉ SACCHARINE COMPANY (1876-1919) [later MANBRÉ SUGAR AND MALT LTD (1919-1926); MANBRÉ AND GARTON LTD (1926-1977)], *Fulham Palace Road, Fulham (1876-1896); Brandenburgh Road [renamed Winslow Road] (1896-), Fulham*
Sugar manufacturers.
Deeds 1829-20th century
Technical papers 20th century.

MORTON AND WATERS, *310 King Street, Hammersmith*
Estate agents.
Ledgers 1985-1989

MOUSELL BROTHERS, *404-406 North End Road, Fulham*
Furniture removers.
Day books, accounts, inventories 1912-1947.

POPE AND SONS, *19, 21 Bridge Road [renamed Hammersmith Bridge Road], Hammersmith*
Carriers.
Ledgers and day books 1832-1923.

R.W. SAVAGE AND COMPANY, *317-325 Putney Bridge Road, Putney, Wandsworth*
Furniture removers.
Day books and accounts 1942-1944.

ROSSER, S. E. [later ROSSER AND RUSSELL LTD (1866-c.1990)], *Northumberland Street, Charing Cross, Westminster (-1874); Queens Wharf, Hammersmith (1874-c.1990)*
Engineers.
Order book 1854-1865.
Deeds and papers 1857-c.1955.

T. CROWTHER AND SON, *282 North End Road, Fulham*
Antique dealers.
Sales and stock books 1938-1948.

W. CHAPMAN AND SONS, *36 Black Lion Lane, Hammersmith*
Builders.
Account books c.1902-1940.

W. GODFREY AND SON, *281 Wandsworth Bridge Road, Fulham; and 54 Inglethorpe Street, Fulham*
Bakers.
Accounts 1923-1979.
Salaries books 1957-1975.

WHITE CITY STADIUM LTD, *Wood Lane, Shepherds Bush, Hammersmith*
Stadium managers.
Events books 1932-1970.

34. FAMILY AND PERSONAL PAPERS AND RECORDS OF PRIVATE ESTATES

BRANDENBURGH, ANSPACH AND BEYREUTH, *Margrave of*, **Christian Frederick Charles Alexander (1736-1806),** *Brandenburgh House, Fulham*
Will and codicil 1793-1796.

BULT, John (1763-c.1824), and Family, Brook Green, Hammersmith; *29 Wigmore Street, Cavendish Square, Westminster*
Butcher.
Correspondence 1796-1846.

BURCHELL, William (-1800) and Matthew (-1828), and Family, *Churchfield House, New Kings Road, Fulham*
Nurserymen.
Wills and related papers 1776-1865.

BURNE-JONES, *Sir* **Edward Coley (1833-1898),** *The Grange, North End Road, West Kensington, Fulham*
Artist.
Letters to physician c.1896-1898.

HOOK, James (1746-1827)
Composer.
Musical manuscript c.1795.

HOOK, Theodore Edward (1788-1841), *Egmont Villa, Fulham*
Writer and wit.
Correspondence 1822-1833 and near-contemporary manuscript copy of diary 1831-1832.
[Original believed to be lost]

LEE, James (1715-1795), and Family, *Vineyard Nursery, Hammersmith*
Nurserymen.
Marriage settlements and trusts 1798-1849.

MORRIS, William (1834-1896), *Kelmscott House, Upper Mall, Hammersmith*
Artist, writer, manufacturer and socialist.
Letters 1885.
Papers of trustees and executors c.1896-1928.

PALMER, John Henry (1861-1952), *52 Walham Grove, Fulham; 20 Parsons Green, Fulham*
Vestryman and councillor, magistrate.
Correspondence, cuttings, invitations, handbills 1874-1928.

PHILIPPART, *Sir* **John (1784?-1874),** *College House, Hammersmith*
Military writer.
Correspondence 1818-1867.

SCOTT, George (1778-1859), and Family, *Ravenscourt, Hammersmith*
Landowner and philanthropist.
Family and estate records 1693-1928.

SULIVAN, Charlotte Antonia (1824-1911), and Family, *Fulham*
Landowner and philanthropist.
Estate records 1806-1912.

35. MANORIAL RECORDS

FULHAM
Minutes, accounts and papers of Homage Jury 1804 -1930.

37. ANTIQUARIANS' COLLECTIONS

37.2. Other collections

BULL, Sir William (1863-1931), *Vencourt, 267-269 King Street, Hammersmith*
Solicitor and M.P.
Correspondence, notes, photographs, cuttings about his involvement in local affairs and other matters
of local historical interest c.1890-1930.

CROKER, Thomas Crofton (1798-1854), and DILLON, T.F *Rosamond's Bower, Parsons
Green Lane, Fulham*
Antiquaries and writers.
Correspondence, notes, engravings and material relating to friends, particularly antiquary Thomas
Baylis (-1880) of The Pryor's Bank, Fulham, and writer and wit Theodore Edward Hook (1788-1841)
of Egmont Villa, Fulham, 1838-1875.

FÈRET, Charles James (1854-1921), *49 Edith Road, West Kensington, Fulham*
Newspaper editor and local historian.
Manuscript of 'Fulham old and new' 1900 plus author's copy of book. Includes unpublished material,
original illustrations and some additions and amendments to the text.

38. COPIES OF SOURCE MATERIAL HELD ELSEWHERE

MORRIS, MARSHALL, FAULKENER AND CO. (1861-1875); [later MORRIS AND CO (1875-)], *Red Lion Square, Holborn*
Minutes 1862-1874.
Letters 1874-1898.
[Originals in Sanford and Helen Berger Collection, U.S.A.]

SCOTT, Jessy Emma (1823-), *Ravenscourt, Hammersmith*
Daughter of George Scott, landowner.
Journal 1843-1844.
[Original in private collection]

WILLIAMS, George H. (-1916), *103 Hazlebury Road, Fulham*
Private, West Yorkshire Regiment, killed in action.
Letters from the Western Front, 1914-1916.
[Originals in private collection]

Uxbridge High Street, 1901

London Borough of Hillingdon

Archives and Local Studies
Central Library
High Street
Uxbridge
Middlesex
UB8 1HD

Tel:
01895 250702

Fax:
01895 811164

E-mail:
archives@hillingdongrid.org

Website:
www.hillingdon.gov.uk/education/library/heritage.htm

Location:
In High Street pedestrianised area.

Nearest stations:
Uxbridge (Metropolitan and Piccadilly Lines), 100 metres.

Parking:
Car parks in town centre, nearest Chimes Shopping Centre.

Days of opening:
Monday - Saturday.

Administrative history:
The London Borough of Hillingdon comprises the former urban district councils of Hayes and Harlington, Ruislip-Northwood, and Yiewsley and West Drayton and the Borough of Uxbridge. Before 1965 the whole area was in the county of Middlesex.

The ancient parishes in the area were: Cowley, Cranford (most in London Borough of Hounslow), Harefield, Harlington, Harmondsworth, Hayes (Norwood part of parish in London Borough of Ealing), Hillingdon, Ickenham, Ruislip and West Drayton. The Uxbridge Local Board of Health [later Uxbridge Urban and Rural Sanitary Authority] was the first local board of health in England when it was created in 1849. It was abolished in 1894 when urban and rural district councils were established.

The Uxbridge Poor Law Union covered most of the present borough apart from Harlington and Harmondsworth parishes which came within the Staines Poor Law Union.

Holdings:

The holdings are based on the former Middlesex County Library local collection and the Uxbridge Library local collection, begun in the 1930s when the Library opened. The holdings cover the area of the present borough, particularly Uxbridge, and the former counties of Middlesex, London and Buckinghamshire, though in less depth.

The majority of the holdings are held in Uxbridge Central Library, though most official archives are kept in store. At least three days notice is required for their producion. The Heritage Service also includes a museum collection most of which is kept in store.

Catalogues and indexes:

General index: Includes entries for printed material, archives and references to some photographs as well as a 'Biographical Index.' Books and pamphlets are also included in the main library catalogue.
Maps index.
Local paintings and prints index.
'McCabe' Index to names listed in sources in Uxbridge Library, London Metropolitan Archives and the Public Record Office.
'Harris' Index to names relating to parish of Ruislip.

Postal and telephone enquiries:

Fees charged for detailed enquiries.

Services:

Photographic service; reproduction fees charged.
Photocopying facilities.
Microfilm/fiche reader/printers.
Loan collections of books.
Loan collection of objects and archive packs for schools; fees charged.
Talks and guided visits to the collection.
Workshops for children and adults.
Publications; list available.

Related collections held elsewhere:

MANOR FARM LIBRARY
Bury Street
Ruislip
Middlesex
HA4 7SU
(tel: 01895 633651)

Collection covering Ruislip area, jointly maintained with the Ruislip, Northwood and Eastcote Local History Society. Among the holdings are the Hoare collection of illustrations and papers of W.A.G. Kemp, a local author.

HAYES AND HARLINGTON LOCAL HISTORY SOCIETY
c/o Mr B.T. White
14 North Way
Uxbridge
Middlesex
(tel: 01895 231218)
Photographs, objects and documents relating to the Hayes and Harlington area.

WEST DRAYTON AND DISTRICT LOCAL HISTORY SOCIETY
c/o Dr R.T. Smith
36 Church Road
West Drayton
Middlesex
(tel: 01895 442610)
Photographs and documents relating to the West Drayton area, including items relating to the manor of Colham.

1. BOOKS, PAMPHLETS AND PERIODICALS

Histories of the area and books about Middlesex, London and neighbouring areas in Buckinghamshire and Hertfordshire. Books about or connected to local people. Holdings are heavily biased towards former borough of Uxbridge. Approximately 10,000 items.

Journals of local history societies and other local groups. Parish magazines and periodicals concerned with local history and genealogy.

Victoria County History:
Middlesex vol. 3 - Cowley, Cranford, West Drayton, Hanwell, Harefield, Harlington.
Middlesex vol. 4 - Harmondsworth, Hayes, Hillingdon, Ickenham, Ruislip, Uxbridge.

3. NEWSPAPERS

Three days notice required for hard copies. No photocopying allowed from bound volumes.

BUCKINGHAMSHIRE ADVERTISER 1861, 1869, 1871-1890, 1914-1915, 1918-1933, 1940-1966. *Uxbridge edition.*

MIDDLESEX AND BUCKS ADVERTISER 1891-1918; continued as MIDDLESEX AND BUCKS ADVERTISER AND COUNTY GAZETTE 1919 to date.

UXBRIDGE GAZETTE 1893, 1903-1917.

UXBRIDGE REVIEW 1899-1905.

SOUTHALL, NORWOOD GAZETTE 1902, 1905, 1909, 1911-1912, 1921-1923.

YIEWSLEY-WEST DRAYTON REVIEW 1904.

RUISLIP-NORTHWOOD COURIER 1908-1918, 1920-1921.

TRIBUNE 1949-1950; continued as WEEKLY POST 1950-1978.

HAYES CHRONICLE 1959-1975.

HILLINGDON MIRROR 1964-1983.

HAYES NEWS 1969-1971, 1975, 1978-1982.

HILLINGDON LEADER 1983 to date.

4. CUTTINGS COLLECTIONS

12 volumes of cuttings, 1943 to date, originally from a variety of sources but latterly mainly from local papers. Indexed in Local History General Index.
48 volumes of cuttings compiled by previous authorities, c.1910-1950s.

5. DIRECTORIES

5.2 London, county and general directories

BERKSHIRE
Kelly's.
1939.

BERKSHIRE, BUCKINGHAMSHIRE AND OXFORDSHIRE
Kelly's.
1883.

BUCKINGHAMSHIRE
Kelly's.
1911, 1931, 1935, 1939.

ESSEX, HAMPSHIRE, HERTFORDSHIRE, KENT, MIDDLESEX, SURREY, SUSSEX AND
WILTSHIRE
Robson's commercial directory of eight counties.
1838, 1839.

ESSEX, HERTFORDSHIRE AND MIDDLESEX
Kelly's.
1910.

MIDDLESEX
Kelly's.
1871, 1878, 1890, 1898, 1926, 1933, 1937.

MIDDLESEX
Home Counties.
1933.

5.3 Local directories

EALING AND HANWELL
Kemp's.
1962, 1965-1971, 1975.

HARROW
Kelly's.
1915, 1929.

HARROW
Kemp's.
1962-1975 (gaps).

HAYES AND HARLINGTON
Kemp's.
1965-1976.

HOUNSLOW, HESTON AND ISLEWORTH
Kemp's.
1964, 1966, 1968-1975 (gaps).

NORTHWOOD, EASTCOTE AND RUISLIP
Rawlinson's.
1923.

PINNER
Kelly's.
1929-1931, 1933, 1934, 1936-1939.

UXBRIDGE
Lake's.
1840-1865 (gaps).

UXBRIDGE
Brown's.
1867.

UXBRIDGE
Cackett's almanac.
1867.

UXBRIDGE
Bealby's.
1869, 1870, 1875.

UXBRIDGE
Morleys.
1871.

UXBRIDGE
Lucy's (from 1887, Lucy and Birch's).
1874, 1887-1896, 1899-1900, 1902.

UXBRIDGE
Eele's.
1876, 1877, 1881.

UXBRIDGE
Hetherington's 'Marvel'.
1878.

UXBRIDGE
King's 'Gazette'.
1887-1904, 1907, 1908, 1913, 1916, 1923-1925, 1928-1933.

UXBRIDGE
Routleff's.
1928.

UXBRIDGE
Kemp's.
1950-1977.

5.4 Telephone directories

5.4.2. Local areas

HILLINGDON
1970 to date.

UXBRIDGE
1962-1970 (gaps).

WEST MIDDLESEX
1954, 1968-1970.

6. ELECTORAL REGISTERS

MIDDLESEX
1838.

MIDDLESEX: UXBRIDGE DIVISION
1889-1914 (gaps).

HAYES AND HARLINGTON
1938 to date.

RUISLIP-NORTHWOOD
1920-1927, 1929 to date.

UXBRIDGE
1921-1931, 1965 to date.

7. ILLUSTRATIONS

Paintings and prints 18th century to date, including portraits and works by local artists in Museum collection. Uxbridge Panorama, two pen and ink rolls of each side of Uxbridge High Street, possibly by William Burgiss c.1800.

About 10,000 illustrations, mainly photographs; most 20th century, but including some, particularly of Uxbridge, are earlier. About a third relate to Uxbridge. Arranged topographically and then subdivided by subject.

About 10,000 glass negatives, from the Uxbridge Gazette, dating from c.1900 to 1975.

8. MAPS

8.1 General maps

The earliest detailed map is a copy of John Rocque's Middlesex 1754. About 900 maps mainly covering the present borough but also including London, Middlesex and Buckinghamshire from 17th century to date including C. Greenwood's Middlesex 1819.

Enclosure maps for Cowley, Harefield, Harlington, Harmondsworth, Hayes, Ickenham, Ruislip, Uxbridge and West Drayton. Farm and estate plans of Denham, Buckinghamshire, pre-1740; Colham Green, Hillingdon, 1767; Harefield 1771; Hayes 1790; Ickenham 1774; Little Hillingdon, Hillingdon, 1797; and Ruislip 1770, 1778.

8.2 Ordnance Survey maps

6 INCHES: 1 MILE (1:10,560); 1: 10,000 (approx. 6 inches: 1 mile)
1866-1883, 1899, 1920, 1934, 1938, 1947, 1951, 1960, 1970 (incomplete).

25 INCHES: 1 MILE; 1: 2,500 (approx. 25 inches: 1 mile)
1866, 1897, 1914, 1934, 1959, 1970s (incomplete).

1: 1,1250 (approx. 50 inches: 1 mile)
1962, 1976, 1980s (incomplete). Copies of current edition in main library.

10 FEET: 1 MILE
1866. Uxbridge township.

9. AUDIO-VISUAL ITEMS

30 reels of films of civic events 1960s.
Videos, including programmes of local interest recorded from the television. They include the *Uxbridge Bed Race* 1984, 1985 and *This is St Giles Ickenham* 1985.

Records, tape recordings and CDs of local choirs and bands; also of civic ceremonies.
6 oral history tape recordings made by the Uxbridge Local History Society.

10. COLLECTIONS OF MUSEUM OBJECTS

Large collection including archaeological finds, social and domestic items, a fire engine and a milk float. Objects are put on display in the Central Library.

11. LOCAL AUTHORITY RECORDS AND RECORDS OF PREDECESSOR AUTHORITIES

Most local authority archives are kept in store. At least three days notice is required for their producion.

11.1 County councils

MIDDLESEX COUNTY COUNCIL
Education Committee:
>Hayes and Harlington Divisional Education minutes 1948-1957, 1963-1965.
>North West Thames Area Divisional Executive:
>>Minutes 1945-1965.
>>Sub-committee minutes 1919-1965.
>>Letter books 1930s.

Education Department:
>Abbotsfield, Swakeleys, Harefield and Vyners Schools Grouped Governing Body minutes 1959-1965.
>Greenway, Evelyns, Bishopshalt and Townmead Grouped Governing Body minutes 1961-1965.
>Ruislip-Northwood Group of Secondary Schools minutes 1959-1965.
>Uxbridge Group of Council Schools minutes 1910-1945.
>Yiewsley-West Drayton Group of Council Schools minutes 1904-1905.
>[See pp.189-191 for archives of Middlesex County Council schools]

Library Committee:
>Hayes-Harlington District:
>>Minutes 1933-1966.
>>Other records 1932-1966.

Ruislip-Northwood District:
>   Minutes 1937-1967.
>   Other records 1930s-1966.
Uxbridge District:
>   Reports and minutes 1922-1965.
>   Other records 1930s-1965.
Yiewsley-West Drayton District:
>   Minutes 1931-1938.
>   Other records 1931-1969.
Other records 1922-1964.

11.2 Hayes and Harlington Urban District area

CRANFORD PARISH COUNCIL
Parochial Committee minutes 1884-1930.
Parish Council minutes 1884-1930.
Parish Meeting minutes 1895-1930.

HARLINGTON PARISH COUNCIL
Vestry minutes 1862-1929.
Parish Council minutes 1894-1930.
Other records 1889-1929.

HAYES PARISH COUNCIL
Parish Council minutes 1864-1904.
Parish Meeting minutes 1864-1904.
Overseers' accounts 1844-1848.
Rate assessments and valuation lists 1827, 1842-1844, 1865, 1893, 1897.

HARLINGTON BURIAL BOARD
Minutes 1869-1895.

HAYES AND HARLINGTON URBAN DISTRICT COUNCIL [Formerly HAYES URBAN DISTRICT COUNCIL until 1930]
Council minutes 1904-1965 (gaps).
Officers' reports 1925-1965.
Committee minutes:
>   Air Raid Precautions Committee 1938-1939.
>   Allotments Committee 1924-1956.
>   Appointments Committee 1939-1941.
>   Building Committee 1947-1956.
>   Catering Committee 1946-1956.
>   Cemetery Committee 1930-1939.
>   Central Purchasing Committee 1946-1956.
>   Charter Committee 1938-1939.

Civic Centre Site Committee 1950-1955.
Civil Defence Committee 1939-1956 (gaps).
Community Centre Committee 1938-1939.
Community Feeding, Billeting and Rehousing Committee 1941-1946.
Education Committee 1944-1965.
Entertainment Committee 1948-1956.
Establishment Committee 1947-1956.
Finance Committee 1934-1938, 1946-1956.
Fire Brigade Committee 1939-1942.
General Purposes Committee 1930-1956.
Housing Committee 1939-1956.
Parks and Open Spaces Committee 1935-1956.
Plans and Town Planning Committee 1937-1947.
Prevention of Accidents Committee 1938-1956.
Public Health and Housing Committee 1919-1956.
Rating Committee 1927-1946.
Sewerage Committee 1928-1929.
Town Planning Committee 1914-1956.
Wood End Park Estate Committee 1946-1949.
Works Committee 1904-1927.
Works, Sewerage and Allotments Committee 1931-1956.
Year books 1920-1965.
Abstract of accounts 1927-1964.
Medical Officer of Health reports 1905-1964.
Treasurer's Department records 1921-1924, 1931-1964.
Rate assessments, valuation lists and other rating records 1913-1965.
Other records 1930-1965.

11.3 Ruislip-Northwood Urban District area

RUISLIP PARISH COUNCIL
Parish Council minutes 1895-1904.
Parish Meeting minutes 1894-1904.
Rate assessments 1886, 1889-1891, 1902.
Other records 1894-1904.

RUISLIP-NORTHWOOD URBAN DISTRICT COUNCIL
Council minutes 1904-1965.
Committee minutes:
 Allotments Committee 1948-1963.
 Buildings Committee 1949-1962.
 Civil Defence Committee 1943-1956.
 Civil Relations Committee 1954-1963.
 Development Committee 1937-1939.
 Estates Committee 1939-1962.

Finance Committee 1934-1962.
Fire Brigade and Air Raid Precautions Committee 1938-1940.
Highways Committee 1934-1963.
Housing Committee 1932-1936, 1946-1965.
Housing and Public Health Committee 1937-1946
Licensing Committee 1948-1953.
Lido Committee 1951-1962.
Parking Sub-committee 1962-1964.
Planning Sub-committee 1955-1963.
Public Health Committee 1904-1905, 1934-1936, 1946-1963.
Rating Committee 1929-1963.
Staff Establishment Committee 1934-1963.
Town Planning Committee 1939-1963.
Urban Horticulture Committee 1948-1962.
Year books 1919-1965.
Medical Officer of Health reports 1905-1918, 1957-1963.
Treasurer's Department records 1920-1922, 1933-1935, 1947-1965.
Rate assessments and other rating records 1914-1965.
Other records 1904-1965.

11.4 Uxbridge Borough area

COWLEY PARISH COUNCIL
Parish Council minutes 1894-1929.

HAREFIELD PARISH COUNCIL
Parish Council minutes 1894-1929.
Rate assessments and valuation lists 1877-1924 (gaps).

HILLINGDON PARISH
Ratebooks and valuation lists 1860-1897.
[See also p.188]

HILLINGDON EAST PARISH COUNCIL
Parish Council minutes 1895-1926.
Rate assessments and valuation lists 1895-1901, 1904, 1914, 1920.
Other records 1895-1899.

HILLINGDON WEST PARISH COUNCIL
Valuation list 1919.

ICKENHAM PARISH COUNCIL
Parish Council minutes 1894-1929.
Valuation lists 1901-1913.

HILLINGDON BURIAL BOARD
Minutes 1854-1937.
Other records 1865-1939.

UXBRIDGE DISTRICT BOARD OF HEALTH
Minutes 1856-1894.

UXBRIDGE RURAL DISTRICT COUNCIL
Council minutes 1895-1929.

UXBRIDGE BOROUGH [Formerly UXBRIDGE URBAN DISTRICT COUNCIL until 1955]
Council minutes 1895-1964.
Committee minutes:
    Air Raid Precautions Committee 1938-1946.
    Allotments Committee 1950-1963.
    Civil Defence Committee 1951-1962.
    Establishment Committee 1953-1955.
    Finance Committee 1904-1962.
    Housing Committee 1921-1963.
    Joint Works Committee 1947-1956.
    Local Safety Committee 1950-1962.
    Maternity and Child Welfare Committee 1924-1928.
    Public Health Committee 1928-1965.
    Rating and Valuation Committee 1927-1953.
    Redevelopment Committee 1954-1962.
    Road Safety Committee 1962-1965.
    Streets, Works and Drainage Committee 1948.
    Works and Planning Committee 1919-1964.
Year books 1914-1965.
Medical Officer of Health reports 1895-1965 (gaps).
Planning Department:
    House plans for Yiewsley and West Drayton 1900-1926.
Public Health Department:
    Canal boats registers 1913-1951.
    Canal boats certificates of registration 1941-1958.
Rate assessments 1865-1964 (gaps).
Other records 1886-1964.

11.5 Yiewsley and West Drayton Urban District area

HARMONDSWORTH PARISH COUNCIL
Parish Council minutes 1888-1930.
Burial Ground Committee 1938.
Rate assessments and valuation lists 1863-1930.
Other records 1900-1930.

WEST DRAYTON PARISH COUNCIL

Parish Council minutes 1927-1929.
Rate assessments and other rating records 1914, 1919.
Accounts 1915-1927.

YIEWSLEY PARISH COUNCIL

Parish Council minutes 1896-1911.
Rate assessments and valuation lists 1902, 1903, 1906, 1908-1912, 1927.
Other records 1896-1910.

YIEWSLEY AND WEST DRAYTON URBAN DISTRICT COUNCIL [Formerly YIEWSLEY URBAN DISTRICT COUNCIL (-1930)]

Council minutes 1911-1965.
Committee minutes:

      Air Raid Precautions Committee 1938-1939.
      Allotments Committee 1934-1948.
      British Restaurant Committee 1942-1945.
      Cemetery and Burial Ground Committee 1937-1948.
      Children's Safety Committee 1937-1943.
      Civil Defence Committee 1939-1945.
      Finance Committee 1922-1948.
      Fire Brigade Committee 1930-1941.
      Fuel Advisory Committee 1939-1948.
      General Purposes Committee 1929-1948.
      Housing Committee 1922-1948.
      Lighting Committee 1936.
      National Fitness Committee 1938.
      Plans Committee 1929-1931.
      Public Health Committee 1911-1948.
      Rating and Valuation Committee 1927-1948.
      S.S.A.F., Welfare, Aid to Russia Committee 1941.
      Staff Committee 1943-1948.
      Stay at Home Holiday Committee 1942.
      Streets and Works Committee 1911-1948.
      Supplies Committee 1934-1938.
      Town Planning Committee 1937-1948.
      Whitley (Joint Works) Committee 1936-1948.

Medical Officer of Health reports 1958-1963.
Treasurer's Department records 1911-1965.
Rate assessments 1911-1965.
Other records 1911-1963.

11.6 London Borough of Hillingdon

Council minutes 1964 to date.
Joint Reorganisation Committee records 1963-1964.
Committee minutes 1971 to date (gaps).
Year books and diary 1965 to date.
Annual reports 1965 to date.
Annual accounts 1964 to date.
Revenue and capital estimates 1964 to date.
Medical Officer of Health reports 1965-1973.
Education Department:
 School governing bodies minutes 1974-1993.
Planning Department:
 Plans of schools, council, offices, housing estates etc. 1869-1971.
Rate assessments and valuation records 1965 -1973.

12. LOCAL RECORDS OF CENTRAL GOVERNMENT

INLAND REVENUE
Cautionary traders licences register 1923-1928.
Duties on land values [Domesday Survey] 1910. Volumes covering most the present London Borough of Hillingdon.

13. RECORDS OF OTHER PUBLIC AUTHORITIES

POST OFFICE
Establishment books (Uxbridge area) 1914-1966.

UXBRIDGE CITIZENS ADVICE BUREAU
Day books 1949-1972.

UXBRIDGE POOR LAW UNION
Copies of orders relating administration of Union 1839-1895.
Records of Bartram Lodge, Harlington Road, Hillingdon [Children's home]:
 Matron's log book 1928-1936.
Ruislip Overseers of the Poor records:
 Minutes 1911-1927.
 Reports 1895-1898.
Yiewsley Overseers of the Poor records:
 Minutes 1913-1929.
 Accounts 1896-1929.

16. RECORDS OF PARISHES

ST JOHN HILLINGDON
Vestry minutes 1919-1923.
Parochial Church Council minutes 1920-1936.
Vestry order books 1806-1894 (gaps).
Churchwardens' accounts 1749-1771, 1857-1872.
Poor law records:
> Overseers' accounts 1779-1894.
> Apprenticeship books 1724-1799.
> Other records 1758-1810, 1850-1891.
Charities records 1839-1897.
Rate assessments 1695-1862.
Other records 1816-1832, 1857-1956.

ST MARGARET UXBRIDGE
Vestry minutes 1828-1837.
Rate assessments 1802-1818, 1838, 1840.

17. RECORDS OF NON-ANGLICAN PLACES OF WORSHIP

17.1 Non-conformist churches

OLD MEETING CONGREGATIONAL CHURCH [later amalgamated with PROVIDENCE CHAPEL], *High Street, Uxbridge, Middlesex*
Baptism registers 1935-1940.
Church Meeting minutes 1831-1962 (gaps).
Deacons' Meeting minutes 1912-1962.
Sunday School minutes 1869-1954 (gaps).
Other records 1822-1828, 1835-1838, 1894-1911, 1914-1962.

PROVIDENCE CONGREGATIONAL CHURCH, *The Lynch, Uxbridge, Middlesex*
Baptism, marriage and burial registers 1789-1855.
Annual reports and accounts 1884-1912 (gaps).
Other records 1893-1962 (gaps).

SOCIETY OF FRIENDS, *York Road, Uxbridge, Middlesex*
Women's Meeting minutes 1849-1965.
Other records 1691-1960.

21. RECORDS OF HOSPITALS, ASYLUMS AND DISPENSARIES

ROYAL SOCIETY FOR THE PREVENTION OF CRUELTY TO ANIMALS: YIEWSLEY AND WEST DRAYTON CLINIC, *Yiewsley, Middlesex*
Cash book 1947-1957.

23. RECORDS OF SCHOOLS AND COLLEGES

BELMONT ROAD SCHOOL, *Uxbridge, Middlesex*
Minutes 1903-1911.
[Part of the archives of Middlesex County Council]

BISHOPSHALT SCHOOL, *Royal Lane, Hillingdon, Middlesex*
Governors' minutes 1932-1944.
Fees book 1933-1945.
[Part of the archives of Middlesex County Council]

COWLEY ST LAWRENCE CHURCH OF ENGLAND SCHOOL, *Worcester Road, Cowley, Middlesex*
Attendance registers 1960-1961, 1970-1971.
[Part of the archives of Middlesex County Council]

DAMIEN SCHOOL, *Pembroke Road, Ruislip, Middlesex*
Attendance registers 1944-1965.

DAWLEY INFANTS SCHOOL, *Dawley Road, Hayes, Middlesex*
Log books 1897-1920.
[Part of the archives of Middlesex County Council]

HAREFIELD SCHOOL. *High Street, Harefield, Middlesex*
Minutes 1905-1944.
Admission register 1891-1908.
[Part of the archives of Middlesex County Council]

HAREFIELD HOSPITAL SCHOOL, *Harefield, Middlesex*
Admission register 1975.
Attendance registers 1977-1980.
Log books 1920-1980.
[Part of the archives of Middlesex County Council]

HARLINGTON AND HARMONDSWORTH SCHOOLS, *Middlesex*
Managers' Minutes 1929-1945.
[Part of the archives of Middlesex County Council]

HARLINGTON NATIONAL SCHOOL, *Harlington, Middlessex*
Minutes 1903-1914.
[Part of the archives of Middlesex County Council]

HARMONDSWORTH COUNCIL SCHOOL, *Harmondsworth, Middlesex*
Minutes 1903-1906.
[Part of the archives of Middlesex County Council]

HAYES COUNCIL SCHOOL, *Clayton Road, Hayes, Middlesex*
Minutes 1906-1934.
Managers' minutes 1938-1945.
Log book 1906-1931.
[Part of the archives of Middlesex County Council]

HILLINGDON AND COWLEY BOYS SCHOOL, *Hillingdon Road, Hillingdon, Middlesex*
Minutes 1903-1928.
[Part of the archives of Middlesex County Council]

HILLINGDON AND DRAYTON BRITISH SCHOOL, *Hillingdon, Middlesex*
Reports 1829-1833.

HILLINGDON COUNCIL SCHOOL, *Uxbridge Road, Hillingdon, Middlesex*
Minutes 1924-1945.
[Part of the archives of Middlesex County Council]

HILLINGDON NATIONAL SCHOOL, *Hillingdon, Middlesex*
Minutes 1902-1940.
[Part of the archives of St John Hillingdon]

HILLINGDON ST ANDREW SCHOOL, *Nursery Way, Uxbridge, Middlesex*
Minutes 1903-1936.
[Part of the archives of Middlesex County Council]

ICKENHAM SCHOOL, *Ickenham, Middlesex*
Managers' minutes 1929-1945.
Log books 1873-1929.
[Part of the archives of Middlesex County Council]

RUISLIP COUNCIL SCHOOL [later RUISLIP MANOR SCHOOL], *Eastcote Road, Ruislip, Middlesex*
Minutes 1927-1977.
[Part of the archives of Middlesex County Council]

SOUTHBOURNE SCHOOL, *Southbourne Gardens, Ruislip, Middlesex*
Log book 1939-1986.
Parent Teachers' Association minutes 1955-1963.
[Part of the archives of Middlesex County Council]

TOWNFIELD SCHOOL, *Central Avenue, Hayes, Middlesex*
Registers c.1930-1981.
Log books 1931-1972.
[Part of the archives of Middlesex County Council]

UXBRIDGE COUNTY SCHOOL, *Greenway, Uxbridge, Middlesex*
Minutes 1907-1952.
[Part of the archives of Middlesex County Council]

UXBRIDGE FREE SCHOOL, *Uxbridge, Middlesex*
Accounts and reports 1810-1834.

UXBRIDGE ST MARGARET SCHOOL, *New Windsor Street, Uxbridge, Middlesex*
Minutes 1903-1920.
[Part of the archives of Middlesex County Council]

UXBRIDGE SCHOOL OF INDUSTRY FOR GIRLS, *Belmont Road, Uxbridge, Middlesex*
Reports 1810-1824 (gaps).

WEST DRAYTON CHURCH OF ENGLAND SCHOOL, *Station Road, West Drayton, Middlesex*
Admission registers 1902-1905, 1935-1941, 1946.
Log book 1909-1946.
Other records c.1939, 1941, 1947.
[Part of the archives of Middlesex County Council]

YIEWSLEY COUNCIL SCHOOL, *St Stephen's Road, Yiewsley, Middlesex*
Minutes 1905-1906.
[Part of the archives of Middlesex County Council]

For archives of governing bodies see also p.181.

27. RECORDS OF FIRE AND SALVAGE BRIGADES

HARMONDSWORTH AND WEST DRAYTON VOLUNTEER FIRE BRIGADE
Minutes 1908-1916
Fire report books 1904-1911, 1930.
Other records 1932-1937.

UXBRIDGE VOLUNTEER FIRE BRIGADE
Minutes 1871-1883, 1895-1915.
Fire report books 1864-1884.
Rules and regulations 1871.

28. RECORDS OF MILITARY AND ARMED BODIES

MIDDLESEX REGIMENT [DUKE OF CAMBRIDGE'S OWN] THIRD VOLUNTEER BRIGADE, *Uxbridge, Middlesex*
No.11 Platoon register 1917.
Photographs 1918.
Uniforms 1890-1950.

UXBRIDGE VOLUNTEER INFANTRY
Minutes 1830.
Other records 1831, 1837, 1838, 1899.

29. RECORDS OF ASSOCIATIONS, CLUBS AND SOCIETIES

ANCIENT ORDER OF FORESTERS: COURT (OLD TREATY HOUSE) NO. 2006, *Uxbridge, Middlesex*
Records 1856-1882 (gaps).

EASTCOTE PARK RESIDENT'S ASSOCIATION
Records 1937-1989.

EASTCOTE WOMEN'S INSTUTUTE
Minutes 1925-1975.
Other records 1928-1979.

FIRST COWLEY WOLF-CUB PACK
Log book 1931-1935.

GLEDWOOD RESIDENTS ASSOCIATION, *Hayes, Middlesex*
Minutes 1969-1975.

HAREFIELD READING CLUB
Book list 1911.

HAYES AMALGAMATED CHARITIES
Accounts 1907-1942.

HAYES AND HARLINGTON ARTS COUNCIL
Minutes 1962-1971.
Correspondence 1965-1970.

HAYES AND HARLINGTON OLD PEOPLE'S WELFARE COMMITTEE
Accounts 1959-1992.
Other records 1948-1989.

HILLINGDON ENVIRONMENTAL ACTION PARTY
Constitution 1973.

HILLINGDON FRIENDLY SOCIETY
Rules 1817.

ICKENHAM AND SWAKELEYS HORTICULTURAL SOCIETY
Minutes 1943-1969.
Other records 1936-1992.

ICKENHAM [formerly SWAKELEYS] RESIDENTS' ASSOCIATION
Minutes 1934-1966.

MIDDLESEX CONSERVATIVE ASSOCIATION: UXBRIDGE BRANCH
Minutes 1870-1906.

MIDDLESEX [formerly UXBRIDGE; HILLINGDON] SHOW SOCIETY
Records 1932-2000.

NORTHWOOD RIFLE CLUB
Minutes 1911-1929.

LORD OSSULTON'S CHARITY, *Uxbridge, Middlesex*
Apprenticeship indentures 1827-1904.

RUISLIP CENTRAL ALLOTMENT SOCIETY, *Manor Farm, Ruislip, Middlesex*
Manor Farm Pig Club records 1941-1944.

RUISLIP RESIDENTS' ASSOCIATION
Minutes 1924-2001.
Other records 1926-1976.

UNITED NATIONS ASSOCIATION: UXBRIDGE BRANCH
Newsletters 1959-1970.

UXBRIDGE AND DISTRICT AGRICULTURAL ASSOCIATION: HORTICULTURAL SECTION
Accounts 1933-1939.

UXBRIDGE AND DISTRICT ARCHAEOLOGICAL SOCIETY
Minutes 1936-1940.

UXBRIDGE AND DISTRICT BOY SCOUTS ASSOCIATION
Records 1940-1945.

UXBRIDGE AND DISTRICT DRAMA FEDERATION
Minutes 1949-1951.

UXBRIDGE AND HILLINGDON BAND
Records 1906-1935.

UXBRIDGE AUXILIARY BIBLE SOCIETY
Annual meeting records 1810-1834.

UXBRIDGE AUXILIARY HIBERNIAN SOCIETY
Report 1827.

UXBRIDGE BOOK SOCIETY
Minutes 1811-1836.
Laws and catalogue 1830.

UXBRIDGE CO-OPERATIVE PARTY
Minutes 1960-1975.

UXBRIDGE CO-OPERATIVE WOMEN'S GUILD
Minutes 1960-1975.

UXBRIDGE CRICKET CLUB
Cuttings 1885-1888.

UXBRIDGE DISTRICT COUNCIL OF SOCIAL SERVICE
Minutes 1948-1951.
Other records 1947-1952.

UXBRIDGE LABOUR PARTY GROUP: SOUTH WARD
Minutes 1951-1973.

UXBRIDGE LABOUR PARTY: WOMEN'S SECTION
Minutes 1966-1973.

UXBRIDGE LADIES BIBLE SOCIETY
Reports 1822-1829.

UXBRIDGE LOCAL HISTORY AND ARCHIVES SOCIETY [formerly UXBRIDGE URBAN DISTRICT COUNCIL ARCHIVES COMMITTEE]
Minutes 1949-1970.
Other records 1971.

UXBRIDGE YOUNG MEN'S IMPROVEMENT SOCIETY
Magazines 1846-1853.

UXBRIDGE YOUNG MEN'S LITERARY INSTITUTE
Rules 1899.

WEST DRAYTON LITERATURE GROUP
Minutes 1968-1976.

31. RECORDS OF BUSINESS ASSOCIATIONS AND MARKET EXCHANGES

UXBRIDGE CHAMBER OF TRADE
Minutes 1923-1949.
Executive Committee minutes 1923-1934, 1954-1974.

33. RECORDS OF BUSINESSES

BELL PUNCH CO., *Uxbridge, Middlesex*
Ticket machine manufacturers.
House magazine 1927-1931.

BELLS ASBESTOS, *Harefield, Middlesex*
Photographs 1914.

BROWNIE, J., *Uxbridge, Middlesex*
Sail cloth and twine maker.
Ledger 1833.

CARTER, William G., *Northwood, Middlesex*
Chemist.
Prescription books 1938-1961.

DAINTY, J. AND SIMPSON, F., *Uxbridge, Middlesex*
Dentists.
Records 1873-1903 (gaps).

EVES, W. L., *Uxbridge, Middlesex*
Architect.
Building plans for Uxbridge area 1894-1920.

GRAINGE AND CO., *Uxbridge, Middlesex*
Ironmongers.
Records 1798-1891.

HARVEY AND GREEN, *Uxbridge, Middlesex*
Solicitors.
Bills 1908-1910.

HETHERINGTON AND SON, *Uxbridge, Middlesex*
Grocers.
Ledger 1856-1863.

KING AND HUTCHINGS, *Uxbridge, Middlesex*
Printers.
Ledger 1902-1913.

NICHOLLS FAMILY, *Uxbridge, Middlesex*
Butchers.
Records 1886-1952.

UXBRIDGE CORN EXCHANGE COMPANY, *Middlesex*
Minutes 1859-1886.
Other records 1859-1876.

UXBRIDGE OLD BANK, *Middlesex*
Accounts 1892-1902.

UXBRIDGE SAVINGS BANK, *Middlesex*
Minutes 1816-1837.

W. HERON AND SON, *Uxbridge, Middlesex*
Sun Fire Insurance agents.
Records 1867-1920.

WOODBRIDGE AND SONS, *Uxbridge, Middlesex*
Solicitors.
Records 1904-1940.

34. FAMILY AND PERSONAL PAPERS AND RECORDS OF PRIVATE ESTATES

MINET FAMILY
Estate papers 1699 to 20th century.

35. MANORIAL RECORDS

COLHAM, *Hillingdon, Cowley and West Drayton, Middlesex*
Quit rent book and abstract of Court books 1788.
[Other records 1681-1888 held by the West Drayton and District Local History Society. Main archive at London Metropolitan Archives, 40 Northampton Road, London EC1R 0AB]

COWLEY PEACHEY, *Cowley, Middlesex*
Court Baron 1636-1846.
[Main archive at London Metropolitan Archives, 40 Northampton Road, London EC1R 0AB]

RUISLIP, *Middlesex*
Court Baron 1710, 1750.
View of Frankpledge. Undated.
[Main archive at Kings College, Cambridge]

UXBRIDGE MANOR, *Middlesex*
Market charter (Basset's grant) 1188.
Court Baron 1728.
Surveys 1636 (copied 1700), 1809.
Other records 1359-1729, 1802, 1855.
[Main archive at London Metropolitan Archives, 40 Northampton Road, London EC1R 0AB]

36. MANUSCRIPTS AND MANUSCRIPT COLLECTIONS

36.1 Literary manuscripts

DRUETT, W.W.
'Hayes and West Drayton through the ages', undated.

HUTSON, Giles
'Recollections of Uxbridge', 1886. Notes of articles published in the Middlesex Advertiser.

JARVIS, L. D.
'Chronicles of Uxbridge 1084-1697', undated.

JARVIS, L. D.
'Free church history of Uxbridge', 1953. Manuscript and galley proofs.

JARVIS, L. D.
'Magistrates of Harefield', 1965. Published in London and Middlesex Historian, no.1, 1965.

JARVIS, L. D.
'The story of Harefield', 1967. Published in Harefield Month, February - December 1967.

JARVIS, L. D.
'The story of Harefield House', 1970. Published 1982.

STRUTT, Thomas
'Peregrinations of a kiddy', c.1873.

37. ANTIQUARIANS' COLLECTIONS

37.2 Other collections

CHALLONER, E.
Photographs of Uxbridge and district up to 1956.

CUTHBERTSON, Elona (-1992)
Notes on Harefield.

DAVENPORT, Percy
Notes on manorial records.

EDWARDS, Francis
Ephemera relating to Northwood 1902-1937.

LE MESSURIER, Colin (-1995)
Notes on Denham, Buckinghamshire.

London Borough of Hounslow

Hounslow, Heston, Osterley, Isleworth, Cranford, Bedfont, Feltham and Hanworth areas (HO):

Local Studies Service
Hounslow Library
CentreSpace
Treaty Centre
High Street
Hounslow
Middlesex
TW3 1ES

Tel:
0845 456 2800

Website:
www.hounslow.info/localstudies

Location:
In Treaty Centre, off High Street.
Lift to all floors.

Nearest stations:
Hounslow Central (Piccadilly Line) 300 metres; Hounslow (South West Trains) 600 metres.

Parking:
Multi-storey car park with lift to Treaty Centre.

Days of opening:
Open by appointment.

Brentford and Chiswick areas (CH):

Local Studies Service
Chiswick Library
Duke's Avenue
London
W4 2AB

Tel:
020-8994 1008

Location:
Off Chiswick High Road. No lift to reference library and local studies room on 1st floor.

Nearest stations:
Turnham Green (District Line) 500 metres; Chiswick (South West Trains) 1200 metres.

Parking:
3 disabled spaces; parking in surrounding streets (meters, pay and display).

Days of opening:
Open by appointment.

Administrative history:
The London Borough of Hounslow comprises the former boroughs of Brentford and Chiswick, Heston and Isleworth, and Feltham Urban District Councils. Before 1965 the whole area was in the county of Middlesex.

The ancient parishes within the borough were: Chiswick, Cranford (part in London Borough of Hillingdon), Ealing (Old Brentford part of parish), East Bedfont, Feltham, Hanwell (New Brentford part of parish), Hanworth, Heston and Isleworth. Most of the parishes of Ealing and Hanwell are in the London Borough of Ealing. Improvement Commissioners were created for Chiswick in 1858, and local boards were established for various areas in the 1870s and 1880s. These were abolished in 1894 when urban and rural district councils were established.

The Brentford Poor Law Union covered the parishes of Chiswick, Brentford, Isleworth and Hounslow (parish created in 1836). The Staines Poor Law Union covered the parishes of East Bedfont, Cranford, Feltham and Hanworth.

Holdings:
The Local Studies Department was established in 1965, but the existing collections were not amalgamated. Holdings exceed 22,000 items, most of which are at Chiswick and Hounslow.

Catalogues and indexes:
Author, title and subject indexes to books, pamphlets, maps and illustrations (CH) (HO). Brentford and Chiswick special indexes include: street indexes to early rate books and electoral registers (CH); name and classified index to Brentford Urban District Council deeds (CH).

Postal and telephone enquiries:
Research charges may apply, details on request.

Services:
Photographic service; reproduction fees may apply.
Photocopying facilities.
Microfilm and microfiche reader/printers.
Talks, fees charged.
Publications on sale at all libraries.

Related collections held elsewhere:

GUNNERSBURY PARK MUSEUM
Gunnersbury Park
Acton
London
W3 8LQ
(tel: 020-8992 1612)
Social and local history museum administered jointly by the Boroughs of Ealing and Hounslow.

HOGARTH'S HOUSE
Hogarth Lane
Great West Road
Chiswick
London
W4 2QN
(tel: 020-8994 6757)
Home of William Hogarth for the last 15 years of his life. Collection of prints relating to him.

1. BOOKS, PAMPHLETS AND PERIODICALS

Books, pamphlets and ephemera on the history of the borough, London and Middlesex. Biographies of those connected with the area. Parish magazines, school journals, publications from local residents and community groups, and periodicals concerned with archaeology and local history.

Victoria County History:
Middlesex vol. 2 - Feltham, Bedfont and Hanworth
Middlesex vol. 3 - Heston and Isleworth
Middlesex vol. 7 - Chiswick and Brentford

2. SPECIAL COLLECTIONS OF PRINTED MATERIAL

CHISWICK PRESS
700 books published by the press 1809-1852 (CH).

HOGARTH COLLECTION
Prints by William Hogarth (1697-1764), books by and about him; including the Crickitt collection of Hogarth prints, early 19th century (CH).

PENDLEBURY COLLECTION
Books on mathematics by Charles Pendlebury (1854-1941), Master at St Paul's School (CH).

PHILIP NORBURY COLLECTION
A selection of works from the printing firm in Brentford High Street produced c.1775-c.1834 (CH).

TRIMMER COLLECTION
Children's stories and books about the setting up of schools of industry and associated teaching practices by Sarah Trimmer (1741-1810) (CH).

3. NEWSPAPERS

MIDDLESEX CHRONICLE 1860-1870 (gaps), 1870 to date (HO).
Subject index 1870 to date (HO).

MIDDLESEX INDEPENDENT 1883-1895; 1896-1962 (some vols available depending on condition) (HO).

CHISWICK TIMES 1895-1927; continued as BRENTFORD AND CHISWICK TIMES 1927-1983; continued as BRENTFORD, CHISWICK AND ISLEWORTH TIMES 1983 to date (CH).
Subject index 1895 to date (CH).

CHISWICK NEWS 1901-1902 (CH).

ACTON AND CHISWICK EXPRESS 1902-1916 [also called CHISWICK EXPRESS or THE EXPRESS] (CH).

CHISWICK DISTRICT POST 1911-1913 (CH)

ACTON GAZETTE 1895-1931 (CH).

CHISWICK AND BRENTFORD GAZETTE 1972-1988 (CH).

EVENING MAIL 1974-1982 (HO).

HOUNSLOW INFORMER 1977 to date (HO).

HOUNSLOW, FELTHAM AND HANWORTH TIMES 1987 to date (HO).
Subject index 1987 to date (HO).

HOUNSLOW RECORDER 1988-1999 (HO).

4. CUTTINGS COLLECTIONS

5 volumes covering Chiswick c.1897-1953 (CH). 8 volumes for Cranford, Heston, Hounslow, Isleworth and Osterley c.1900-1965 (HO).

5. DIRECTORIES

5.2 London, county and general directories

LONDON
Pigot and Co's London and Provincial Commercial.
1823/24, 1826/27 (HO); 1839/40 (Middlesex section) (CH) (HO).

LONDON
Post Office.
1833, 1837 (vol. 2) (HO).

LONDON
Post Office Suburban (Kelly's).
1894 (CH).

LONDON
Post Office (Kelly's).
1900, 1913, 1933-1999 (CH).

MIDDLESEX
Robson's.
1837 (HO).

MIDDLESEX
Kelly's.
1862, 1867, 1874, 1878, 1882, 1890 (HO); 1914, 1922, 1926, 1933, 1937 (CH) (HO).

MIDDLESEX AND SURREY
Kelly's.
1852, 1899, 1903 (HO).

MIDDLESEX
Thomason's West Middlesex Year Book.
1864-1899, 1901-1966 (gaps) (HO).

5.3 Local directories

BEDFONT, FELTHAM, STAINES
Caxton's Directory.
1914 (HO).

BRENTFORD
Mason's Court Guide and General Directory.
1853 (CH) (HO).

BRENTFORD
W. H. Jackson.
1872, 1877 (CH).
Includes Isleworth.

BRENTFORD
County of Middlesex Independent Directory of Middlesex.
1888, 1896, 1899 (CH).

BRENTFORD AND CHISWICK
Classified guide to Business and Trade [Blue Book].
1951-1968 (gaps) (CH).

CHISWICK
Kelly's.
1915, 1916, 1919-1940 (CH).
Covers Acton, Gunnersbury and Chiswick 1915-1927; covers Gunnersbury, Chiswick and Brentford 1928-1940.

EALING
Kelly's.
1887/88, 1888/89, 1893/94-1913, 1917, 1918, 1920-1921, 1924 (CH).
Covers Acton, Chiswick, Ealing, Gunnersbury and Hanwell (and Brentford 1897-) 1887-1913; covers Ealing, Hanwell, Brentford and Southall 1917-1924.

HESTON AND ISLEWORTH
Thomason's.
1936, 1939 (HO).

HOUNSLOW
Thomason's.
1887, 1913, 1915, 1919-1927 (gaps) (HO).

HOUNSLOW
Hounslow and District Commercial Guide.
1931 (HO).

HOUNSLOW
Classified guide to Business and Trade [Blue Book].
1949-1970 (gaps) (HO).

HOUNSLOW
Kemp's.
1964-1976 (gaps) (HO).

RICHMOND
Whetstone and Co. Court Guide.
1848 (CH).
Includes Brentford.

5.4 Telephone directories

5.4.2 Local areas

EALING, HOUNSLOW AND DISTRICT
1953-1969 (gaps) (HO).

HOUNSLOW, HESTON, ISLEWORTH
1926, 1931 (HO).

HOUNSLOW AND DISTRICT
1951-1953 (HO).

HOUNSLOW
1971 (HO), 1976 to date (CH) (HO).

5.4.3 Yellow pages

LONDON (NORTH WEST)
1976 to date (CH) (HO).

LONDON (SOUTH WEST)
1969 (HO), 1976-1982 (CH); 1983 to date (CH) (HO).

6. ELECTORAL REGISTERS AND POLL BOOKS

BRENTFORD
1929, 1931-1935, 1937-1939 (CH).

BRENTFORD AND CHISWICK
1945-1965 (CH).

CHISWICK
1909-1919 (gaps), 1920-1939 (CH).
Jurors' lists.
1900-1905, 1915-1918, 1920, 1921 (CH).

HESTON AND ISLEWORTH
1840 (copy of list of property voters in parish) (HO).

HESTON AND ISLEWORTH
1912/13, 1915/16, 1926-1965 (HO).

MIDDLESEX
Poll books (taken at Brentford).
1705, 1710, 1802 (CH).

MIDDLESEX: BRENTFORD DIVISION
1890-1897, 1899-1914 (CH).

LONDON BOROUGH OF HOUNSLOW
1965 to date (HO); 1965 to date (Brentford and Isleworth only) (CH).

7. ILLUSTRATIONS

Paintings and prints of the borough from the 18th century to date (CH) (HO). Photographs from 1850 to date (CH) (HO). Collection of slides (CH) (HO).

8. MAPS

8.1 General maps

County maps from the late 16th century including John Rocque's maps 1741-1745 and 1754 and Thomas Milne's land use map of London and environs (1800) (CH) (HO).

Copies of Moses Glover's map of Isleworth Hundred 1635. A. Basset's plan of the processional boundaries of Ealing parish, which covers Old and New Brentford, 1777 and photocopies of 1822 and 1836 editions (CH).

Enclosure schedules and award maps for the parishes of East Bedfont 1813, Feltham 1800, Hanworth 1800, Heston 1813, and Isleworth 1813 (HO). Tithe schedules and award maps for the parishes of Chiswick 1847, Ealing (including Old Brentford) 1839, and New Brentford 1838 (CH); East Bedfont 1840 (HO). Tithe map for Isleworth 1850, published 1871. Numerical and occupier index for tithe award maps.

8.2 Ordnance Survey maps

Sheets covering the entire borough are held at Hounslow Library. Maps for Brentford and Chiswick are also held at Chiswick Library.

6 INCHES: 1 MILE (1: 10,560); 1: 10,000 (approx. 6 inches: 1 mile)
1869, 1894-1897, 1911-1913, 1932-1935, 1973.

25 INCHES: 1 MILE; 1: 2,500 (approx. 25 inches: 1 mile)
1865, 1894-1897, 1913-1915, 1934-1935, 1957-1970.

60 INCHES: 1 MILE (1: 1,056)
1848/50. Brentford and Chiswick. Skeleton survey (HO).
1867, 1936. Kew and the Glebe Estate to the Hammersmith boundary (CH).
1894/95. Brentford and Chiswick (CH), Brentford and Isleworth (HO).

1: 1,250 (approx. 50 inches: 1 mile)
1965 to date.

9. AUDIO-VISUAL ITEMS

Films include: Platt's Stores Sports Day at Hounslow 1912; the opening of Gunnersbury Park Museum 1926; Brentford and Chiswick War Weapons Week 1941; Dr Henry Mandiwall's training films of Heston Fire Station drill c.1938; Hounslow Hospital's emergency procedure after a bombing incident c.1941; Alderman, G.N. Shackleton, J.P., (Mayor of Heston and Hounslow 1940-1941) and his family; Heston and Isleworth Borough Council's films on local events during World War II; and the Coronation celebrations 1953, from which two videos have been compiled. More recent films include: Syon House, Isleworth c.1950; Holy Trinity Church, Hounslow 1963; the London Borough of Hounslow c.1968; and the future of Chiswick Town Hall c.1975 (HO).

Oral history tapes of memories c.1900-1940 (HO).

11. LOCAL AUTHORITY RECORDS AND RECORDS OF PREDECESSOR AUTHORITIES

11.1 Brentford and Chiswick Borough area

CHISWICK PARISH
Vestry minutes 1777-1817, 1836-1896 (CH).
Select Vestry overseeing Workhouse minutes 1822-1825, 1828-1832 (CH).
Churchwardens' accounts 1856-1871 (CH).
Highway, paving and watching records:
    Minutes 1836-1858 (CH).

Accounts 1828-1858 (CH).
Letterbook 1838-1846 (CH).
Parish patrolmen's notebook 1827-1828 (CH).
Poor Law records:
Overseers' minutes 1887-1888, 1895-1912 (CH).
Overseers' accounts 1736-1766 (CH).
Overseers' receipts and payments 1884-1900 (CH).
Chiswick Lighting District records:
Inspector's minutes 1856-1857 (CH).
Turnham Green Lighting District records:
Inspector's minutes 1843-1857 (CH).
Treasurer's accounts 1852-1858 (CH).
Rate assessments 1736-1766, 1776-1803, 1834, 1844-1856 (CH).
Census returns: heads of households 1801 (CH).
Charity records 1633-1886, 1914-1925 (CH).
Parish pensions 1825-1828.

OLD BRENTFORD PARISH
Vestry minutes 1895-1927 (CH).

BRENTFORD LOCAL BOARD
Board minutes 1874-1894 (CH).
Ledgers 1874-1894 (CH).
Rate assessments 1875-1894 (CH).
Other records 1883-1894 (CH).

CHISWICK BURIAL BOARD
Cash book 1888-1895 (CH).
Ledgers 1888-1897 (CH).
Register of fees c.1890 (CH).

CHISWICK IMPROVEMENT COMMISSIONERS
Commissioners' minutes 1858-1885 (CH).
Committee minutes:
Drainage Committee 1882-1883 (CH).
Finance Committee 1874-1891 (CH).
Works Committee 1874-1887 (CH).
Other records 1858-1896 (CH).

CHISWICK LOCAL BOARD
Board minutes 1885-1893 (CH).
Committee minutes:
Audit and Finance Committee 1891-1896 (CH).
Law and Parliamentary Committee 1885-1896 (CH).
Works Committee 1884-1896 (CH).
Annual reports and accounts 1888-1894 (CH).

Medical Officer of Health reports 1888-1896 (CH).
Ledgers 1881-1894 (CH).
Vestry Hall accounts 1877-1899 (CH).
Private street improvements accounts 1883-1884 (CH).

CHISWICK SCHOOL BOARD
Board minutes 1872-1903 (CH).
Finance Committee minutes 1896-1922 (CH).
Ledgers 1873-1903 (CH).
Other records 1899-1926 (CH).

NEW BRENTFORD BURIAL BOARD
Minutes 1854-1927 (CH).
Register of mortgages 1883-1909 (CH).

BRENTFORD URBAN DISTRICT COUNCIL
Council minutes 1895-1927 (gaps) (CH).
School Managers' minutes 1912-1927 (CH).
Medical Officer of Health reports 1892-1928 (CH).
Library Committee:
    Reports 1890-1907 (CH).
    Letter book 1911-1913 (CH).
Ledgers 1895-1926 (CH).
Rate assessments 1894-1926 (CH).

CHISWICK URBAN DISTRICT COUNCIL
Council minutes 1901-1927 (CH).
Committee minutes:
    Public Health minutes 1901-1928 (CH).
Annual reports 1895-1909 (CH).
Abstract of accounts 1923-1926 (CH).
Medical Officer of Health reports 1900-1927 (gaps) (CH).
Pensions Committee letter book 1918-1924 (CH).
Private street improvements accounts 1895-1902 (CH).
Ledgers 1895-1926 (CH).
Rate assessments 1895-1928 (CH).

BRENTFORD AND CHISWICK URBAN DISTRICT COUNCIL
Council minutes 1928-1932 (CH).
Abstract of accounts 1928-1932 (CH).
Medical Officer of Health reports 1927-1928, 1930-1931 (CH).
Rate assessments 1928-1932 (CH).

BRENTFORD AND CHISWICK BOROUGH COUNCIL
Council minutes 1932-1965 (CH).
Abstract of accounts 1932-1939, 1948-1964 (CH).

Annual estimates 1935-1965 (gaps) (CH).
Medical Officer of Health reports 1931, 1934-1938, 1945-1964 (CH).
Record of incidents caused by enemy action 1939-1945 (CH).
Rate assessments 1932-1961.

11.2 Feltham Urban District Council area

EAST BEDFONT PARISH
Minutes 1894-1929 (HO)
Rate assessments 1914, 1927, 1929 (HO).
List of persons who received coal 1888-1901 (HO).

FELTHAM PARISH
Vestry minutes 1808-1863 (HO).
Minutes 1895-1904 (HO).
Rate assessments 1855, 1864 (HO).

HANWORTH PARISH
Minutes 1894-1930 (HO).
Rate assessments 1914, 1927-1930 (HO).

FELTHAM URBAN DISTRICT COUNCIL
Includes Bedfont and Feltham from 1930.
Council and Committee minutes 1904-1965 (HO).
Rate assessments 1904-1905, 1914, 1928-1929, 1930 (Hanworth); 1931 (Bedfont and Feltham); 1939-1946, 1950, 1960, 1963-1965 (Bedfont, Feltham and Hanworth). (HO).

11.3 Heston and Isleworth Borough area

HESTON PARISH
Vestry minutes 1710-1812 (HO).
Overseers' minutes 1904-1906 (HO).
Rate assessments 1869, 1890 (HO).

ISLEWORTH PARISH
Vestry minutes 1655-1927 (HO).
Board of Feoffees minutes 1813-1836, 1847-1855 (HO).
Re-assessment Committee minutes 1831-1852 (HO).
Churchwardens' accounts 1651-1740 (HO).
Highway and paving records:
      Board of Surveyors' minutes 1851-1874 (HO).
      Surveyors' accounts 1723-1826 (HO).
Poor law records:
      Overseers' accounts 1701-1833 (HO).

Settlement examinations 1779-1801, 1814-1830 (HO).
Workhouse minutes 1773-1836 (HO).
Rate assessments 1651-1866 (HO).

HESTON SCHOOL BOARD
Minutes 1879-1903 (HO).
Report book 1885-1903 (HO).

ISLEWORTH SCHOOL BOARD
Minutes 1893-1903 (HO).

HESTON AND ISLEWORTH URBAN DISTRICT COUNCIL
Council and Committee minutes 1904-1932 (HO).
Joint Isolation Hospital Committee with Borough of Richmond [South West Middlesex Hospital] minutes 1911-1925 (HO).
Rate assessments 1914-1928 (gaps) (HO).

HESTON AND ISLEWORTH BOROUGH COUNCIL
Council and Committee minutes 1932-1965 (HO).
Rate assessments 1939-1946, 1950, 1960, 1963-1965 (HO).

11.4 London Borough of Hounslow

Council and Committee minutes 1965 to date (HO).

12. LOCAL RECORDS OF CENTRAL GOVERNMENT

INLAND REVENUE
Duties on land values [Domesday Survey] 1909. Volumes covering the present London Borough of Hounslow (HO).

13. RECORDS OF OTHER PUBLIC AUTHORITIES

BRENTFORD POOR LAW UNION
Minutes 1923-1930 (HO).
Letter book 1840-1846 (HO).

BRENTFORD TURNPIKE TRUST
Minutes 1717-1802, 1820-1826 (CH).
Mortgages of tolls 1769-1781 (CH).
Accounts 1717-1826 (CH).
Other records 1787-1873 (CH).

GRAND JUNCTION CANAL [now known as GRAND UNION CANAL]
Boat certificates 1889-1895, 1903-1937 (CH).
Canal Boat register 1879-1936 (CH).
Other records 1879-1906, 1923-1951 (CH).

ISLEWORTH TURNPIKE TRUST
Minutes 1767-1826 (HO).
Accounts 1779-1836 (HO).
Other records 1767-1826 (HO).
[Part of the records of Isleworth parish]

14. RECORDS OF COURTS OF LAW

BRENTFORD MAGISTRATES COURT
Alehouse registers 1907-1919 (CH).
Beerhouse licence registers 1907-1919 (CH).
Registers also cover other areas in Middlesex.

16. RECORDS OF PARISHES

ALL SAINTS ISLEWORTH
Registers:
       Baptism 1566-1852 (HO).
       Marriage 1566-1895 (HO).
       Burial 1566-1879 (HO).
Banns 1754-1816, 1896-1911, 1920-1928 (HO).

ST JOHN THE BAPTIST ISLEWORTH
Minutes re building of new church 1853-1858 (HO).

ST LAWRENCE NEW BRENTFORD
New Brentford was formerly part of Hanwell parish.
Vestry minutes 1814-1864 (CH).
Chapel wardens accounts, assessments and orders of vestry 1615-1814 (CH).
Highway, paving and watching records:
    Constable's rates and accounts 1688-1710 (CH).
Inspector of Gas Lighting records:
    Minutes 1864-1874 (CH).
Correspondence 1861-1874 (CH).
Rate assessments and valuation lists 1617-1671, 1714-1722, 1729-1817 (CH).
Census returns 1810: heads of households (CH).
Other records 1700s, 1816-1865 (CH).

17. RECORDS OF NON-ANGLICAN PLACES OF WORSHIP

17.1 Non-conformist churches

BRENTFORD WESLEYAN METHODIST CHAPEL, *Brentford, Middlesex*
Collection books 1868-1911 (CH).

BRENTFORD TOWN MISSION, *Brentford, Middlesex*
Minutes 1908-1933.

21. RECORDS OF HOSPITALS, ASYLUMS AND DISPENSARIES

CHISWICK HOSPITAL, *Chiswick Mall, Chiswick, Middlesex*
Ward registers 1918-1923, 1929-1935 (CH).
Children's Ward registers 1921-1934 (CH).
X-ray register 1924-1935 (CH).
Operations registers 1919-1935 (CH).

23. RECORDS OF SCHOOLS AND COLLEGES

ACTON AND CHISWICK POLYTECHNIC [CHISWICK POLYTECHNIC from 1928], *Bath Road, Chiswick, Middlesex*
Minutes 1899-1915, 1923-1944 (CH).
Prospectuses 1901-1906, 1913-1982 (CH).

ACTON AND CHISWICK PUPIL TEACHER CENTRE, *Chiswick, Middlesex*
Minutes 1904-1908 (CH).

BEDFONT AND HATTON SCHOOL, *Hatton Road, Bedfont, Middlesex*
Minutes 1903-1921 (HO).

BEDFONT INFANTS SCHOOL, *Hatton Road, Bedfont, Middlesex*
Minutes 1906-1910 (HO).

BEDFONT OLD SCHOOLS, *Hatton Road, Bedfont, Middlesex*
Minutes 1952-1965 (HO).

BEDFONT SCHOOLS, *Hatton Road, Bedfont, Middlesex*
Minutes 1921-1945 (HO).

BELMONT BOYS SCHOOL, *Belmont Road, Chiswick, Middlesex*
Log books 1927-1930 (CH).

BELMONT SENIOR MIXED SCHOOL, *Belmont Road, Chiswick, Middlesex*
Log books 1930-1949 (CH).

BOSTON MANOR SCHOOL, *Boston Manor School, Brentford, Middlesex*
Log books 1940-1961 (CH).

BRENTFORD BRITISH SCHOOL, *High Street, Brentford, Middlesex*
Managers' minutes 1843-1873 (CH).
Log books 1863-1906 (CH).

BRENTFORD END SCHOOL, *Isleworth, Middlesex*
Log books 1925-1935 (HO).

BRENTFORD SENIOR BOYS SCHOOL, *Clifden Road, Brentford, Middlesex*
Log book 1930-1948 (CH).
Honours book 1930-1957 (CH).

BRENTFORD TEMPORARY INFANTS SCHOOL [later CLIFDEN ROAD SCHOOL],
Upper Butts, Brentford, Middlesex
Log books 1907-1940 (CH).

CHISWICK CHARITY SCHOOL [later CHISWICK NATIONAL SCHOOL], *St Nicholas*
Church, Chiswick, Middlesex
Minutes 1860-1878 (CH).
Accounts 1706-1879 (CH).

CHISWICK COUNTY SCHOOL FOR GIRLS, *Burlington Lane, Chiswick, Middlesex*
Governors' minutes 1917-1919 (CH).

EALING ROAD HANDICRAFT CENTRE
Log books 1907-1931 (CH).

FELTHAM COUNCIL SCHOOLS
Management Board minutes 1912-1945 (HO).

FELTHAM SCHOOL, *Feltham, Middlesex*
Minutes 1903-1912 (HO).

FELTHAM SECONDARY SCHOOLS
Management Board minutes 1958-1967 (HO).

GLEBE INFANTS SCHOOL, *Glebe Street, Chiswick, Middlesex*
Log books 1883-1947 (CH).

GREEN SCHOOL, *Isleworth, Middlesex*
Minutes 1914-1943 (HO).
Cash book 1940-1953 (HO).

HANWORTH COUNCIL SCHOOLS
Management Board minutes 1903-1945 (HO).

HOGARTH BOYS SCHOOL, *Duke Road, Chiswick, Middlesex*
Log books 1896-1921 (CH).

HOGARTH GIRLS SCHOOL, *Duke Road, Chiswick, Middlesex*
Log books 1863-1927 (CH).

HOGARTH SENIOR BOYS SCHOOL, *Duke Road, Chiswick, Middlesex*
Log books 1921-1940 (CH).

HOGARTH SENIOR GIRLS SCHOOL, *Duke Road, Chiswick, Middlesex*
Log books 1927-1940 (CH).

HOGARTH SECONDARY MODERN SCHOOL, *Duke Road, Chiswick, Middlesex*
Log book 1948-1967 (CH).
Admissions register 1947-1962 (CH).

HOLME COURT SCHOOL, *Twickenham Road, Isleworth, Middlesex*
Founded as a truant school and later an industrial school.
Minutes 1890-1899, 1918-1920 (HO).
Log books 1891-1899, 1908-1920 (HO).

HOUNSLOW POLYTECHNIC, *Hounslow, Middlesex*
Admissions registers 1914-1915, 1917-1921 (HO).

HOUNSLOW SUBSCRIPTION BOYS SCHOOL, *School Road, Hounslow, Middlesex*
Log book 1862-1908 (HO).

HOUNSLOW SUBSCRIPTION GIRLS SCHOOL, *School Road, Hounslow, Middlesex*
Log book 1862-1897 (HO).

HOUNSLOW SUBSCRIPTION INFANTS SCHOOL, *School Road, Hounslow, Middlesex*
Log book 1862-1902 (HO).

HOUNSLOW TOWN BOYS SCHOOL, *School Road, Hounslow, Middlesex*
Log book 1908-1937 (HO).

HOUNSLOW TOWN GIRLS SCHOOL, *School Road, Hounslow, Middlesex*
Log book 1897-1947 (HO).

HOUNSLOW TOWN INFANTS SCHOOL, *School Road, Hounslow, Middlesex*
Log book 1901-1923 (HO).

HOUNSLOW TOWN JUNIOR MIXED AND INFANTS SCHOOL, *School Road, Hounslow, Middlesex*
Fire watching records 1941-1945 (HO).

ISLEWORTH CHARITY SCHOOL [now THE BLUE SCHOOL], *Isleworth, Middlesex*
Minutes 1715-1834, 1855-1869 (HO).
Accounts 1715-1808, 1834-1866 (HO).
Registers 1715-1851 (HO).
Foundation deed [copy] 1715 (HO).

ISLEWORTH COUNTY SCHOOL, *St John's Road, Isleworth, Middlesex*
Minutes 1922-1943 (HO).
Cash book 1940-1952 (HO).

ISLEWORTH GRAMMAR SCHOOL, *St John's Road, Isleworth (-1939); Ridgeway Road, Isleworth, Middlesex (1939-)*
Minutes 1951-1966 (HO).
Scholarship accounts 1924-1966 (HO).
Staff register 1897-1979 (HO).

MIDDLESEX COUNTY COUNCIL TECHNICAL EDUCATION COMMITTEE
Minutes 1893-1919 (CH).
Minutes relate to Chiswick Polytechnic.

NEW BRENTFORD CHARITY SCHOOL, *St Lawrence's Church, Brentford, Middlesex*
Minutes 1703-1714 (CH).

ROTHSCHILD BOYS SCHOOL, *High Street, Brentford, Middlesex*
Log books 1906-1930 (CH).
Honours book 1869-1950 (CH).

ROTHSCHILD GIRLS SCHOOL, *High Street, Brentford, Middlesex*
Log book 1914-1930 (CH).

ROYAL NAVAL FEMALE SCHOOL, *Isleworth, Middlesex*
Ledger 1868-1875 (HO).

ST GEORGE'S BOYS SCHOOL, *Green Dragon Lane, Brentford, Middlesex*
Log book 1893-1905 (CH).

ST GEORGE'S GIRLS SCHOOL, *Green Dragon Lane, Brentford, Middlesex*
Log books 1874-1926 (CH).

ST GEORGE'S INFANTS SCHOOL, *Green Dragon Lane, Brentford, Middlesex*
Log books 1911-1930 (CH).

SPRING GROVE INFANTS SCHOOL, *Isleworth, Middlesex*
Log book 1899-1913 (HO).

SPRING GROVE NATIONAL SCHOOL, *Isleworth, Middlesex*
Boys and Girls Departments' Log books 1888-1924 (HO).

STRAND ON THE GREEN BOYS SCHOOL, *Chiswick, Middlesex*
Log book 1891-1912 (CH).

STRAND ON THE GREEN MIXED SCHOOL, *Chiswick, Middlesex*
Log book 1871-1891 (CH).

TURNHAM GREEN GIRLS SCHOOL, *Horticultural Place, Chiswick, Middlesex*
Log book 1880-1892 (CH).

TURNHAM GREEN INFANTS SCHOOL, *Horticultural Place, Chiswick, Middlesex*
Log book 1862-1896 (CH).

TURNHAM GREEN SPECIAL SUBJECTS CENTRE, *Chiswick, Middlesex*
Log book 1910-1939 (CH).

WORPLE ROAD SCHOOL, *Isleworth, Middlesex*
Minutes 1908 (HO).

28. RECORDS OF MILITARY AND ARMED BODIES

HOUNSLOW BARRACKS, *Beavers Lane, Hounslow, Middlesex*
Orderly books 1798-1800 (HO).

29. RECORDS OF ASSOCIATIONS, CLUBS AND SOCIETIES

BRENTFORD AND CHISWICK LOCAL HISTORY SOCIETY
Records 1958- (CH).

BRENTFORD EVENING TOWNSWOMEN'S GUILD
Committee minutes 1950-1990 (CH).
Meeting records 1950-1990 (CH).

BRENTFORD RIVERSIDE ASSOCIATION
Records 1978-1989 (CH).

CHISWICK GOLF CLUB, *Sutton Court Road, Chiswick, Middlesex*
Records 1894-1907 (CH).

CHISWICK GROUP OF ARTISTS
Minutes 1935-1937.
Visitors book for exhibitions 1937-1938, 1951 (CH).
Cuttings, programmes and photographs c.1920s-1951 (CH).

CHISWICK HORTICULTURAL SOCIETY
Minutes 1938-1958, 1972-1978 (CH).
Show schedules and other records 1950s-1980s (CH).

CHISWICK PROTECTION GROUP
Minutes 1985-1992 (CH).

HOUNSLOW TOC H SOCIETY
Records 1937-1961 (HO).

ST MARY'S SPORTS GROUND, *Osterley, Middlesex*
Records 20th century (HO).

THISTLEWORTH TENNIS CLUB, *Osterley, Middlesex*
Records 20th century (HO).

WEST CHISWICK RESIDENTS ASSOCIATION
Records 1979-1990 (CH).

30. RECORDS OF THEATRES AND CINEMAS

Q THEATRE, *Kew Bridge, Brentford, Middlesex*
Repertory theatre 1924-1956.
Programmes, photographs and other records (CH).

33. RECORDS OF BUSINESSES

BARRATT, W.G., *Chiswick High Road, Chiswick, Middlesex*
Undertakers.
Records of funerals 1828-1903 (CH).

EYDMANN, Henry, *Turnham Green, Chiswick, Middlesex*
Builder.
Ledgers 1863-1870 (CH).

FINNIS, Robert, *Turnham Green, Chiswick; Chiswick, Middlesex*
Attorney.
Records 1815-1844, 1862-1866 (CH).

HOGG AND CLOUSTON, *Ainslie Lodge, Turnham Green, Chiswick; Priory House, Priory Gardens, Chiswick, Middlesex*
Doctors.
Register of patient accounts 1879-1883 (CH).

KEW BRIDGE, *Brentford, Middlesex*
Toll book 1759-1780 (CH).

LONDON, HOUNSLOW AND WESTERN RAILWAY
Records relating to parliamentary case for a railway line from Staines to London 1846 (HO).

MAYNARDS BOAT YARD, *Grove Park Road, Chiswick, Middlesex*
Records c.1871-1939 (CH).

MULLINERS COACH WORKS, *Bath Road, Chiswick, Middlesex*
Photographs of the factory and pre-1914 cars (CH).

TARRY, C.J., *508 Chiswick High Road, Chiswick, Middlesex*
Dentist.
Ledger of treatments and payments 1902-1908 (CH).

35. MANORIAL RECORDS

BOSTON, *New Brentford, Middlesex*
Copy of court proceedings 1692-1842 (CH).

SUTTON COURT, *Chiswick, Middlesex*
Deeds and other records 18th-19th centuries. *Name index.*

37. ANTIQUARIANS' COLLECTIONS

37.2 Other collections

LAYTON COLLECTION

Material covering Kew Bridge, Brentford Ferry, New Brentford, the Layton family and lighterage business. 18th century London theatre playbills, books on British topography and antiquities 16th-19th centuries, prints of London and the Home Counties from 17th century, London and Middlesex maps 16th-19th centuries (HO).

Beating the bounds, Old Brentford, 1911

INDEX